THE SENSITIVE GOURMET

The Sensitive Gourmet

IMAGINATIVE
COOKING
WITHOUT
DAIRY,
WHEAT
OR
GLUTEN

*Antoinette
Savill*

Thorsons
An Imprint of HarperCollins*Publishers*

Thorsons
An Imprint of HarperCollins*Publishers*
77–85 Fulham Palace Road,
Hammersmith, London W6 8JB

Published by Thorsons 1998
1 3 5 7 9 10 8 6 4 2

© Antoinette Savill 1998
© Photographs by John Turner 1998

Antoinette Savill asserts the moral right to
be identified as the author of this work

A catalogue record for this book
is available from the British Library

ISBN 0 7225 3713 1

Printed in Great Britain by The Bath Press, Bath.

Contents

Acknowledgements

First of all I would like to thank Stephen Lawrence for all the help and time he has spent working on this book with me. I couldn't have done it without him. Also Sir Charles Jessell for his advice and encouragement and everybody who has helped me to put this book together over the last two years.

Foreword

Diet is a four letter word, and it is often accompanied by a five letter word: gloom. This is a book to dispel any such ideas of despondency. It is about celebration. There is no reason why people with food intolerance should not enjoy their meals as much as anyone else, provided they follow the advice of people like Antoinette Savill.

She, and I, and, it is estimated, about sixty percent of the world's population, suffer from sensitivity to certain items in their diet. So this book should have a wide appeal to anyone who wants to have a social occasion with a meal that does not leave them, or their guests, feeling ill afterwards.

By careful manipulation, it is always possible to avoid one's worst food antagonists. However, Antoinette Savill makes it a pleasure. Jack Sprat *and* his wife would both be able to come to her parties – and to yours, if you read this book and act upon it. I recommend you to have it in your kitchen, and you will be ready to receive them.

Charles Jessell
Chairman of Governors, 1997–8
The Institute for Optimum Nutrition

Introduction

For many years, people have known that stress, pollution and junk food have taken their toll on our systems. Fortunately as our health improves we become better able to deal with stress. However, the reverse can also be true, so it is vital to stay healthy!

More and more people are being diagnosed as suffering from food intolerances or dietary problems, and are often advised to follow bland, unappetizing diets. Having experienced the misery of such advice and the monotony and frustration of a restrictive diet, I decided to plunder my notes and embark on my fourth cookbook to prove that it is possible to eat exciting food and stay healthy. This book uses intensely flavoured contemporary recipes, so delicious that they will appeal to all who love eating and enjoy uncomplicated cooking!

The many different grains used in these recipes will benefit everybody by helping to vary and balance their fibre intake. For those without dietary problems, all of these recipes can be made using dairy and wheat products and served with normal breads.

Food intolerance is, by its nature, such a complex subject and no two people experience exactly the same intolerance. While nearly all the recipes are dairy or wheat free and so helpful to IBS and ME/chronic fatigue sufferers as well as others, there are plenty of recipes that have no gluten for coeliacs. Please remember that other ingredients included in the recipe may not be suitable for individual intolerance.

Food intolerance can change over time and some people may become less sensitive to certain foods after these have been avoided for a while, and so menu planning can evolve using different recipes in this book.

Even people who do not suffer from the most common food sensitivities may react to the chlorine in tap water and so I recommend that you use filtered or boiled water for cooking and drinking. Finally, the few people who are sensitive to aluminium should obviously not use saucepans made from this metal!

My passion for food comes, essentially, from the intoxicating Mediterranean flavours: ripe and heady smells of fresh herbs, fruit and vegetables that are piled up on market stalls and wicker baskets, displayed casually but always looking glorious and in harmony with their surroundings. Not for me the regimented piles of perfect supermarket fruit and vegetables that all too often have no perceptible aroma but only a flaccid dullness evocative of nothing except the mysteries of science. This cosmopolitan collection of recipes, although at heart European, also has a sprinkling of oriental and Asian influences, whose intriguing ingredients are now available all over the world.

My aim in this book is to use the healthiest food resources we have to promote our own good health and I hope that much relief will be felt by all families and friends who are completely nonplussed when confronted with having to cook for someone with a dietary restriction at a lunch or dinner party. These culinary feasts will, I am sure, restore your enjoyment not merely of cooking but of eating too!

This is not a conventional recipe book nor was it born of an immediate inspiration. The idea eventually crystallized one wet and gloomy afternoon when my winter taste buds needed to be cosseted by combative carrot cake. The consequent challenge of creating a wheat and dairy free cake effectively immersed me into a culinary fervour of researching, writing and testing.

I have chosen both contemporary and old-fashioned recipes that were totally hostile to my dietary needs, and replaced the conventional ingredients with appropriate substitutes, transforming them into tasty and healthy meals for every occasion throughout the year. Sunflower and soya products replace dairy. Corn and rice products replace the starch and cereals that are normally used. These changes need to be enhanced with more intense flavourings to enliven the undistinguished taste of soya.

Social occasions over the past four years for me have been a mixture of stress and anxiety over the inevitable negotiations in order to eat out. Now, however, having covered the fundamental problems associated with juggling ingredients, I can safely and quickly prepare menus to suit even the most restrictive of diets. Medical opinion is now that we all eat far too much wheat, dairy products and sugar, so these recipes will be a healthy change. A lot of problems, I feel, come from the artificial colourings, additives, preservatives, pesticides and chemicals that are mixed with or coated onto many of today's foods. These problems can, of course, be overcome by buying organic food and washing thoroughly or peeling off all the vegetable and fruit skins.

Special diets, if stuck to, can certainly alleviate the symptoms and reintroducing foods after a period of abstinence can be successful, but sometimes, as with a coeliac, it's for life. A little sympathy goes a long way and everybody will appreciate making the effort to provide delicious food that can be enjoyed by all. It is important that you do not try to diagnose or treat yourself: if you are having problems with foods or liquids do seek the advice and help of a good nutritionist, doctor or homeopathic practitioner. This book will help you to avoid certain foods while still letting you enjoy food, but will not cure your intolerance.

The nutritional value of our foods is most important, especially if you are on any restricted diet. Throughout the book, you will find well-balanced menus with plenty of starch, which provides sugar and fibre, to fill you up and make you feel contented. The decrease in consumption of fats will help you achieve and maintain a healthy weight, but I do advise using unsaturated fats that are unhydrogenated which helps considerably in reducing cholesterol and heart disease. Remember it's not the bread that is fattening, but what you spread on it.

Carbohydrates are essential fillers and give you slowly released energy. You can buy very good breads such as (GF) sourdough or corn bread, but take care to read the labels. This applies to everything we buy as, unfortunately, most foods have added sugar, wheat or yeast in them. Our sugar consumption has increased dramatically and we no longer eat enough unrefined foods, which is why I have used such ingredients as brown rice and honey. Once you get used to them you will be struck by the nutty and sweet flavours they impart.

We don't need too much sugar, as it is high in calories and has no protein or vitamins. You quickly notice how the sweetness of fruit and vegetables is intensified once you have removed sugar from your diet.

Cutting out dairy products means losing a lot of protein, especially in the form of cheese. Yoghurt is easier to digest than milk, so some people who cannot tolerate milk may be able to eat yoghurt. In some cases, if these can be tolerated, I have used goat's and sheep's products in recipes. These products now have very sophisticated flavours and textures – quite unlike 10 years ago!

Soya milk is a white liquid made exclusively from soya beans. You can buy it sweetened and with calcium, which helps to improve the taste, but it is still a processed food and so I use it as little as possible. Soya cream adds thickness and richness, but with all the optimism I possess I can't get it to whip up properly. This makes it ineffective as a filler. A more workable solution is to always have a tub of (GF/WF/DF) Swedish glacé or Tofutti ice cream desert that can cunningly be used to fill meringues, roulades or other puddings.

A professional nutritionist has assessed every recipe in this book, so you can be inspired with absolute confidence. However, do please check each recipe before you start planning, shopping or cooking, as it would be extremely annoying to find at the last minute that it is unsuited to your specific needs.

Today's entertaining is all about convenience. We are all subjected to the pressures of everyday life, food fads and advertising. However unrealistic you might think it, take time to regularly relax and enjoy cooking at home as it is immensely satisfying and will have a lasting and beneficial impact on your health, family and friends.

CHAPTER 1

Soups and Starters

Quick Seafood Soup and Rouille

A deep nostalgia for the south of France descends on me each time I make this soup. It reminds me of sun-baked terracotta, wild thyme and chilled rosé wine.

Serves 6

CHEATING ROUILLE
500ml/16fl. oz/2 cups of (DF/GF) mayonnaise
1 large free-range egg yolk
A dash of French mustard and (GF) chilli sauce/oil
Salt and freshly ground black pepper

SOUP
1 large onion, peeled and finely chopped
2 tablespoons of olive oil
4 cloves of garlic, peeled and crushed
2 bay leaves
1 sprig of thyme
195g/6½oz/1 cup of canned tuna fish, drained

800ml/28fl. oz/3 cups of carrot juice
A few drops of (GF) chilli sauce/oil
400g/14oz/2½ cups of frozen seafood cocktail, defrosted
A dash of sherry
1 tablespoon of chopped parsley, to garnish

CROUTONS
(GF) bread
Olive oil
1 clove of garlic peeled and crushed
Thyme
Or ready-made (GF) croûtons

First make the rouille. Mix all the ingredients in a bowl and chill until needed. Store any leftovers in a sealed jar in the refrigerator. (You can use it over the next week.)
Make the croûtons by frying small, crustless cubes of bread in olive oil, garlic and thyme. Drain on absorbent paper and keep warm.
In a large saucepan cook the onion in olive oil, until soft but not brown. Add the garlic and cook for 1 more minute. Add the herbs and then the tuna. Stir and cook for a further minute. Pour in the carrot juice and (GF) chilli sauce/oil. Leave to simmer on a medium heat for 15 minutes. Stir in the seafood and sherry and cook for 1 minute.
Remove from the heat and leave for 3 minutes.
Pour the soup into warm bowls and sprinkle with parsley. Serve with croûtons.
Transfer the rouille to a bowl and serve with the soup.

Cucumber, Coconut and Lime Soup

The transformation that fresh lime produces in any dish is instantaneous, releasing its powerful zest, and lifting the dish from the ordinary to the sublime.

Serves 10

1 small onion, peeled and chopped
4 tablespoons of sunflower oil
2 large cucumbers, peeled, seeded and chopped
2 cloves of garlic, peeled and chopped
600ml/20fl. oz/2½ cups of boiling water with 1 tablespoon of (GF) vegetable stock powder
8 spring onions (scallions), trimmed and chopped
2 red chillies, seeded and chopped

2 lemon grass stalks, chopped
800ml /28fl. oz/3 cups of canned coconut milk
The grated rind and juice of 2 limes
Salt and freshly ground black pepper
200ml/7fl. oz/¾ cup of coconut cream
2 tablespoons of chopped coriander (cilantro) leaves

Cook the onion in half the oil for 5 minutes. Add the cucumbers and garlic and gently cook for 2 minutes.

Add the water and stock powder. Simmer for 15 minutes; cool and liquidize.

Wash the pan and heat the remaining oil. Cook the spring onions (scallions), chillies and lemon grass over a medium heat for 2 minutes.

Stir in the cucumber liquid and add the coconut milk, grated rind and juice of 2 limes. Season to taste with salt and freshly ground black pepper.

Heat through gently for 5 minutes. Allow to cool and then chill until needed.

Stir in the coconut cream to taste, and serve in cold bowls with a sprinkle of chopped coriander (cilantro).

Winter Smoked Bacon Soup

The onset of another wet and windy day lured me to my store cupboard. With nothing more than a can of beans, I decided to conjure up a comforting soup to revive my flagging spirits.

Serves 8

1 large onion, peeled and finely chopped
1 large carrot, peeled and finely chopped
3 tablespoons of olive oil
6 thick slices of rindless smoked back bacon, chopped
4 large cloves of garlic, peeled and crushed
2 bay leaves
1kg 260g/2lb 13oz/6 cups of canned butter (lima) beans (drained), or 500g/16½oz/2½ cups of dried

butter (lima) beans, soaked in water for 5 hours, drained and boiled for 10 minutes
1½ tablespoons of (GF) vegetable stock powder
2 litres/3¼ pints/2 quarts of water
1 tablespoon of chopped parsley
1 tablespoon of chopped sage
Black pepper and grated nutmeg, salt if needed
A few drops of (GF) chilli sauce/oil

Cook the onion and carrot in the oil in a medium saucepan until slightly soft. Add the bacon, followed by the garlic and bay leaves and cook for 3 minutes. Stir in the beans. Pour over the water, add the stock powder and bring to the boil. Add half the chopped parsley and sage, plenty of seasoning and (GF) chilli sauce/oil to taste.

Reduce heat and simmer for 40 minutes. Cool slightly before liquidizing into a smooth purée. Return to the pan and reheat. Serve in warm bowls with the remaining herbs sprinkled over.

Mexican Black Bean Soup

I find black beans culinarily challenging at the best of times – their need for long hours immersed in water had discouraged me from using them, but inspired by one of the great chefs I find that they are indeed a delicacy and well worth the extra effort.
For an authentic Mexican dish serve the soup with Chilli and Herb Corn Bread (see page 115).

Serves 6

1 large onion, peeled and chopped

2 red chilli peppers, seeded and chopped

3 tablespoons of olive oil

250g/9oz/1½ cups of dried black beans, soaked in water overnight and then drained

1 clove of garlic, peeled and crushed

2 litres/3¼ pints/2 quarts of water mixed with 2 tablespoons of (GF) vegetable stock powder

2 celery stalks, trimmed and sliced

2 carrots, trimmed and sliced

2 sprigs of thyme

2 bay leaves

1 teaspoon each of ground cloves and ground mace

Salt and freshly ground black pepper

3 tablespoons of chopped coriander (cilantro) leaves

In a large pan, cook the onion and chilli peppers in the oil for 5 minutes, until soft but not brown. Sprinkle in the black beans and garlic. Pour in the water and stock powder.

Add the celery, carrots, thyme, bay leaves and spices. Season to taste and simmer for 1½ hours, or until the beans are soft. Top up with more water if necessary.

Cool, remove the bay leaves and liquidize. Adjust the seasoning if necessary.

Serve hot with a sprinkling of chopped coriander (cilantro) and slices of Chilli and Herb Corn Bread (*see page 115*).

Pickled Ginger, Lemon Grass and Mussel Soup

The impact of pickled ginger is balanced by the subtleties of fresh lemon grass. I keep both in the fridge for stir-fries and curries.

Serves 6

1 tablespoon of sesame oil

6 spring onions (scallions), trimmed and chopped

1 medium red chilli, seeded and chopped

2 cloves of garlic, peeled and crushed

2 stalks of lemon grass, finely sliced

1kg/2.2lb of prepared fresh (or frozen) mussels in or out of shells

415g/15oz of condensed beef consommé

600ml/20fl. oz/2½ cups of water

145g/5oz of pickled ginger slices, drained

1 teaspoon of (GF) fish sauce (or double up on [GF] soy sauce)

1 teaspoon of dark (GF) soy sauce

Salt and freshly ground black pepper

1 bunch of fresh coriander (cilantro), chopped

Heat the oil in a large pan. Add the onions (scallions), chilli, garlic and lemon grass. Cook for 3 minutes.

Add the mussels, followed by the consommé, water, pickled ginger, (GF) fish sauce and (GF) soy sauce. Season and then simmer for 10 minutes.

Serve the soup immediately in hot bowls and sprinkle with the coriander (cilantro).

Tomato Mousse and Avocado Ceviche

Here, the traditional Mexican mix of tomatoes, avocados, black beans, coriander (cilantro) and limes are put together in a more European way as an ideal starter.

Serves 6

100g/3½oz/½ cup of black beans, soaked in water
   overnight
2 ripe avocados, skinned, stoned and chopped
2 beef tomatoes, skinned, seeded and chopped
1 red chilli, seeded and chopped
1 small red onion, peeled and very finely chopped
The juice of 3 limes, and grated rind of 2 of them
Salt and freshly ground black pepper
2 tablespoons of olive oil
3 tablespoons of coconut cream
1 teaspoon of coriander (cilantro) seeds, crushed
   with a rolling pin
Large bunch of coriander (cilantro) leaves

MOUSSE
Sunflower oil for greasing
700g/24oz/3 cups of tomato passata
(GF) chilli sauce/oil and (GF) Worcestershire sauce
The juice of ½ a lemon
11g/½oz of gelatine
40g/1½oz of rocket (arugula) leaves, washed and
   dried

The day before you need them, cook the beans in boiling water until soft.

To make the ceviche, first drain and then mix the beans in a large bowl with the avocado, tomatoes, chilli, onion, lime juice and zest, seasoning, olive oil, coconut cream, coriander (cilantro) seeds and half of the chopped coriander (cilantro) leaves.

Marinate overnight or for at least 4 hours, turning occasionally.

To make the mousse, grease 6 ramekins with sunflower oil and line each mould with baking parchment (wax paper).

Mix the tomato passata with the chilli and Worcestershire sauce, lemon juice and seasoning to taste.

Dissolve the gelatine by stirring into about 2 tablespoons of boiling water in a cup until it is clear and without any lumps.

Stir this into the tomato mixture and place in the fridge to chill and thicken slightly.

After about 10 minutes, spoon the mousse into each ramekin and level off. Chill until set.

Cut the rocket (arugula) stems in half, and arrange on each plate.

Turn out each mousse onto the plate by briefly dipping the ramekins into a bowl of boiling water.

Remove the paper, spoon the avocado ceviche around the mousse.

Serve with Sesame Corn Crackers (*see page 104*), or Chilli and Herb Corn Bread (*see page 115*).

Potato Skins and Hummus Dip

An almost instantaneous starter at any time of the year. Brilliant for barbecues, hungry teenagers and vegetarians. Use ready-made wafers (chips) (GF/WF/DF) if you are in a real hurry!

Serves 8

Home-made fried potato skin quarters, or
   500g/17oz of (GF/DF) ready-made fried potato
   skins, or 200g/7oz of (WF/GF) ready-made wafers
   (chips)
Salt and freshly ground black pepper
840g/30oz/4 cups of canned chickpeas (garbanzo
   beans), drained
2 tablespoons of light tahini paste

3 large cloves of garlic, peeled and chopped
A few drops of (GF) chilli sauce/oil
The juice of 2 large lemons
297g/10½oz of silken tofu (firm)
At least 3 tablespoons of fresh coriander (cilantro)
   leaves
Cayenne pepper
A little chopped parsley for decoration

Set the oven at 200°C/400°F/Gas mark 6.

Place the potato skins on a non-stick baking sheet and sprinkle with salt and pepper. Then bake in a preheated oven until crispy. Meanwhile, mix the chickpeas (garbanzo beans), tahini, garlic, (GF) chilli sauce/oil, lemon juice, tofu, salt, pepper and coriander (cilantro) leaves together in the food processor until smooth.
Scoop into an attractive bowl. Sprinkle with cayenne pepper and parsley.
Place in the centre of a large oval plate and arrange the potato skins around the dip.
Serve immediately.

Roast Artichoke, Fennel and Onion Salad

Once laborious to peel, Jerusalem artichokes have now been perfected into a less complex shape. I have now been converted to these underrated vegetables as an alternative to potatoes.

Serves 4

500g/17oz of fresh Jerusalem artichokes (washed and peeled and left in a bowl of cold water and a teaspoon of fresh lemon juice to prevent discolouration)

Chilli oil and olive oil

2 heads of fennel, trimmed and quartered

2 large onions, peeled, trimmed and quartered

Salt and freshly ground black pepper

2 cloves of garlic, peeled and crushed

Fresh marjoram

The juice of 1 lemon

Set the oven at 200°C/400°F/Gas mark 6.

Cook the artichokes in boiling water for 10 minutes. Drain and rinse under cold water. Sprinkle a large non-stick baking sheet with the oils. Mix the vegetables together and spread over the sheet. Sprinkle with more of the oils, salt and pepper, crushed garlic and the marjoram. Place the tray in the centre of the oven and roast until golden (about ³/₄–1 hour).
Carefully spoon the vegetables into a salad bowl and sprinkle with the lemon juice. Serve with warm (GF) bread, or cover and chill until needed.

Pumpkin and Cheese Tart

Pumpkins are now widely available and are just as popular in England as in the USA. Here is an interesting new recipe for you to try.

Serves 6

PASTRY
100g/3¹/₂oz/²/₃ cup of brown rice flour
75g/2¹/₂oz/¹/₂ cup of maize flour
75g/2¹/₂oz/¹/₂ cup of porridge oats
¹/₂ teaspoon of salt
110g/4oz/¹/₂ cup of (DF) margarine
1 large free-range egg, beaten
1 tablespoon of olive oil

FILLING
600g/21oz of pumpkin flesh, peeled, seeded and
   sliced into thin wedges

4 tablespoons of olive oil
1 small onion, peeled and sliced
1 teaspoon of fresh thyme leaves
1 clove of garlic, peeled and crushed
Salt and freshly ground black pepper
Grated nutmeg
125g/4¹/₂oz/1 cup of grated goat's or sheep's cheese
250g/8¹/₂oz/2 cups of goat's or sheep's yoghurt
3 large free-range eggs, beaten
A pinch of cayenne pepper and a bunch of lamb's
   lettuce (mâche)

First set the oven at 200°C/400°F/Gas mark 6.

Now make the pastry. Place the flours, oats, salt and margarine in a food processor and mix for a second or two until it resembles fine breadcrumbs. Mix the egg and oil together and pour into the food processor with the machine running.
Turn out the mixture onto a floured board and, with floured hands, bring into a ball of dough. Wrap in clingfilm (plastic wrap) and chill for 30 minutes. Roll out on a floured board and line a 24cm/10" non-stick fluted loose-bottomed flan tin. Prick the bottom with a fork and chill for 1 hour. Line the pastry with greaseproof (wax) paper and ceramic beans and bake for 10 minutes. Remove the balls and paper and bake for a further 25 minutes. Cool until needed.
Turn down the oven to 180°C/350°F/Gas mark 4. Blanch the pumpkin slices in boiling water for 5 minutes until they are softened. Heat half the oil and fry the pumpkin slices for 10 minutes to brown them on each side. Remove from the pan and drain on absorbent paper.
Add the remaining oil and cook the onion with the thyme and garlic, until soft, but not brown. Season with salt, pepper and grated nutmeg and cover the pastry base with the mixture. Arrange the pumpkin wedges on top and all around the flan.
Mix the cheese, yoghurt and eggs together with a little more seasoning and spoon over evenly. Sprinkle with a little cayenne pepper and bake for 45 minutes, or until puffy and firm and the pumpkin is cooked through.
Serve warm, or cold, with lamb's lettuce (mâche), drizzled with virgin olive oil and black pepper.

Sweet Pepper Tart

Grilling (broiling) the peppers is crucial to bring out the intense sweet flavour vital to the success of this tart and other sauces and soups. The skins should blister with black spots before being peeled off.

Serves 6

4 large red peppers, halved and seeded
Olive oil
1 plump clove of garlic, peeled and crushed
1 teaspoon of marjoram leaves
1 teaspoon of balsamic vinegar
225g/8oz/1 cup of soya cream
6 large free-range egg yolks
Salt and freshly ground black pepper

A little caster (superfine) sugar
A few drops of (GF) chilli sauce/oil
Pre-baked (WF/DF) shortcrust pastry case made in a 24cm/10" non-stick loose-bottomed fluted flan tin (see *page 10*)
Cayenne pepper
150g/5oz of lamb's lettuce (mâche)

Set the oven at 200°C/400°F/Gas mark 6.

Brush the peppers with olive oil and grill (broil) until charred and blistered. Leave to cool and then peel off the skin with a sharp knife and discard. Chop up the peppers, and then cook in a tablespoon of oil with the garlic and marjoram for 2 minutes. Add the balsamic vinegar to the pan and cook for 3 minutes.

Put the cream, eggs and cooled peppers in a food processor and blend until smooth. Adjust the seasoning with salt, pepper, sugar and (GF) chilli sauce/oil and blend again. Scrape the mixture into the prepared pastry case. Sprinkle lightly with cayenne pepper and bake for 25–30 minutes or until set.

Serve in warm wedges with a little lamb's lettuce (mâche) sprinkled with olive oil and black pepper around each piece.

Pink Grapefruit and Ginger Salad

Without doubt the easiest and quickest recipe in the book. Ideal for reluctant hosts or hectic hostesses. Ordinary grapefruits are too acidic as a starter, so the pinker the better.

Serves 8

250g/9oz of parsley, trimmed and chopped

Salt and freshly ground black pepper

2 plump cloves of garlic, peeled and crushed

1 teaspoon of balsamic vinegar

6 tablespoons of olive oil

10cm/4" of ginger, peeled

6 large pink/red grapefruit, peeled

40g/1½oz of lamb's lettuce (mâche)

Make the dressing in a large bowl by beating together three quarters of the chopped parsley with seasoning, garlic, vinegar and oil. Grate in all of the ginger. Segment the grapefruit, removing all the pith, skin and pips (seeds) and marinate in the dressing until needed (up to 24 hours). Keep covered in the fridge.

Serve on plates with a bundle of lamb's lettuce (mâche) and crispy warm (GF) bread.

Smoked Mackerel Pâté

This recipe transforms boring old tofu into a delicious pâté. In 60g/2oz of tofu there are 300mg of calcium so it is an excellent alternative to the cheese products we'd normally use.

Serves 6

4 fillets of smoked mackerel, skinned
297g/10½oz of silken tofu (firm)
The juice of ½ lemon
1 teaspoon of (GF/DF) hot horseradish relish or a
 few drops of (GF) chilli sauce/oil

Salt and freshly ground black pepper
Cayenne pepper
Slices of (GF) bread or pure maize corn chips

Put the mackerel, tofu, lemon juice, horseradish or (GF) chilli sauce/oil, salt and freshly ground black pepper into the food processor and process until just smooth.

Spoon into a serving dish. Sprinkle with cayenne pepper and serve with toasted slices of (GF) bread or corn chips, or cover and chill until needed.

Wild Rice and Smoked Trout Blinis

I found it mildly surprising that this recipe actually worked! Its nutty flavour is well matched by the subtleties of smoked trout. This dish is delicious with chilled vodka and will certainly get the party going.

Serves 6 (2 each)

DRESSING	BLINIS
2 tablespoons of capers, drained	75g/2¹/₂oz/¹/₂ cup of well-cooked wild rice
50g/2oz/¹/₂ cup of anchovies, drained and finely chopped	175g/6oz/1¹/₂ cups of buckwheat flour
The juice and rind of 1 large lemon	1 large free-range egg
4 tablespoons of olive oil	300ml/10fl. oz/1¹/₄ cups of sheep's or goat's yoghurt
Salt and freshly ground black pepper	1 teaspoon salt
1 sprig of fresh rosemary leaves, very finely chopped	1 level teaspoon of (GF) baking powder
1 teaspoon of honey	25g/1oz of sunflower oil (and some more for frying)
	¹/₂ teaspoon of bicarbonate of soda (baking soda)
	1 tablespoon of boiling water
4 whole Arbroath smokies/smoked trout	500g/16¹/₂oz/2 cups of Greek set sheep's yoghurt
	2 tablespoons of chopped parsley
	Freshly ground black pepper

Make the dressing first by whisking all of the ingredients in a bowl. Cover and chill in a fridge until needed.

Remove all the skin and bones from the Arbroath smokies and break into attractive pieces. Cover and chill.

Next make the blinis. In a food processor briefly beat the flour, egg, yoghurt, salt, baking powder and oil into a smooth batter. Mix this gently into the rice. Dissolve the bicarbonate of soda (baking soda) with the hot water and stir quickly into the mixture.

Cover the base of a frying pan with oil. Heat the oil until it is hot enough to fry a tablespoon of batter until it sizzles and becomes golden and puffy. Flip the blini over and cook on the other side until golden. Make 12 blinis.

Keep them warm on a dish covered with a clean damp tea towel. Use more oil as necessary. Place a warm blini on each plate. Pile on the smoked trout. Spoon over a blob of yoghurt, sprinkle with parsley and black pepper.

Drizzle the dressing around the blinis and serve immediately.

Warm Scallops and Fennel with Tomato Dill Dressing

Dynamic yet simple is how I prefer my scallops. Briefly cooked so that they still impart the flavour of the ocean – never stewed or frazzled.

Serves 4

4 bulbs of fennel, trimmed and quartered	450g/16oz/4 cups of fresh or frozen, defrosted
Extra virgin olive oil for brushing and serving	scallops (without coral)
½ red onion, peeled and finely chopped	4 tablespoons of tomato passata
1 tablespoon of olive oil	15g/½oz/½ cup of fresh dill, chopped
1 tablespoon of (DF) margarine	Salt and freshly ground black pepper
4 tablespoons of white wine	4 scallop shells, cleaned

First set the oven at 200°C/400°F/Gas mark 6.

Brush the fennel with oil and bake in a hot oven until browned and the edges have softened, about 45 minutes.

Cook the onion in the tablespoon of oil with a little margarine until soft.

Add the wine, cook for another minute and then add the scallops. Cook for a further minute, turning once.

Add the tomato passata and continue to cook for 1 more minute with the dill, salt and pepper.

Spoon the mixture into the shells and serve in the centre of large warm plates surrounded by the fennel quarters.

Drizzle with any remaining sauce and a little extra virgin olive oil, then sprinkle with black pepper.

Crab Mousse with Pear Vinaigrette

The craze for pink peppercorns is no longer with us. Now, of course, they are easily purchased in any reputable supermarket and we no longer have to scour the shelves of smart delicatessens.

Serves 6

11g/½oz of gelatine

2 dressed crabs, fresh or frozen and defrosted

2 tablespoons of (DF/GF) mayonnaise

(GF) chilli sauce/oil to taste

(GF) Worcestershire sauce to taste

The juice of ½ a lemon

Salt and freshly ground black pepper

2 tablespoons of soya cream

1 egg white, stiffly beaten

411g/14½oz/2 cups of pear quarters in natural juices

2 tablespoons of olive oil

The juice of 2 limes

2 teaspoons of pink peppercorns, drained

In a cup, dissolve the gelatine in 3 tablespoons of boiling water and stir until clear and without lumps.

Grease 6 ramekins or moulds. Cut out 6 circles of baking parchment (wax paper) and cover the base of each ramekin.

In a bowl, mix the crab meat, mayonnaise, sauces, lemon juice and seasoning with the cream. Stir in the gelatine, fold in the egg white and spoon the mousse into each mould. Cover with clingfilm (plastic wrap) and chill for 3–4 hours.

When ready to serve, drain the pears and slice up. Turn the mousse onto each plate by dipping the ramekins or moulds into a little boiling water.

Remove the baking parchment (wax paper). Arrange the pear slices around each mousse. Mix the oil, lime juice and peppercorns with salt and pepper, and drizzle over the pears.

Smoked Salmon Turbans

Smoked salmon and the Christmas festivities seem unequivocally bound together. Unmistakably luxurious, it's a special treat meriting little or no intervention from its natural state. However, this recipe does help a little go a long way.

Serves 8

15g/¹/₂oz of gelatine
550g/19oz of salmon fillet, all bones and skin removed
A few slices of lemon
Salt and freshly ground black pepper
297g/10¹/₂oz of tofu (set firm)
1 teaspoon of tomato purée (paste)
2 tablespoons of lemon juice

A few drops of (GF) Tabasco sauce/chilli oil
3 teaspoons of dry sherry
460g/16oz of sliced smoked salmon
2 packets of watercress, trimmed
Extra virgin olive oil
2 large lemons, cut into 8 wedges

In a cup, dissolve the gelatine in 3 tablespoons of boiling water and stir until clear and without lumps. Meanwhile, wrap the salmon in foil with a little water, a few slices of lemon, salt and pepper. Poach for 15 minutes.

Open the foil and leave to cool. Flake the fish with the juices into a bowl and then briefly process together the tofu, fish and juices in a food processor with the tomato, lemon juice and Tabasco. Then stir in the gelatine and beat thoroughly until pink, creamy and smooth. Transfer to a bowl and fold in the sherry with a metal spoon and then line each ramekin or mould with clingfilm (plastic wrap). Line the clingfilm (plastic wrap) with salmon slices, making sure that there are no holes and that there is an overlap to fold over to encase the mousse.

Divide the mousse between the ramekins, and then smooth over and seal up with the overlapping salmon. Cover with clingfilm (plastic wrap) and chill for 4 hours or more. Turn out onto the centre of each plate, surround with watercress and drizzle with the oil and pepper. Serve each turban with a wedge of lemon and a plate of thinly sliced Cumin Seed and Rye Bread (not GF) (*see page 116*) or (GF) bread of your choice.

Avocado and Fresh Salmon Corn Meal Pancakes

These pancakes are ideal for breakfast with bacon and eggs on top, or scrambled eggs and smoked salmon for special occasions. They are also superb with avocado and bacon, fresh prawns or crab as a starter or even a light lunch.

Serves 6

450g/16oz of fresh skinless and boneless salmon
   fillet cut into 2cm/³/₄" cubes
250ml/8fl. oz/1 cup of fresh lime juice
2 fresh chillies, seeded and finely chopped
Salt and freshly ground black pepper
2 ripe avocado pears, peeled and stones removed
1 very large tomato, skinned and finely chopped

CORN MEAL PANCAKES
110g/4oz/³/₄ cup of sifted fine corn meal
110g/4oz/³/₄ cup of sifted white rice flour
3 heaped teaspoons of (GF) baking powder
1 teaspoon of salt
Freshly ground black pepper
2 eggs, lightly beaten
250ml/8fl. oz/1 cup of goat's yoghurt

Oil for frying
3 tablespoons of freshly chopped coriander
   (cilantro) leaves

Start 2–24 hours before eating. In a china or glass bowl, marinate the fish in the lime juice with the chillies and seasoning until it is opaque. Keep chilled and cover with clingfilm (plastic wrap).

When you are ready to make the pancakes, chop up the avocados into cubes and add to the lime juice with the tomato.

Just before serving, make the pancakes. Mix the dry ingredients together in one bowl and the liquid ingredients in another, then quickly but thoroughly stir them together.

Heat a little oil in a non-stick frying pan and make 6 pancakes, using about 3 spoonfuls of batter for each one.

Cook over a medium heat for 3–4 minutes, turning once, until cooked right through and golden on both sides.

Keep the pancakes warm in a low oven until they are all prepared.

To serve, place each pancake on a hot plate. Drain the salmon and avocado mixture and arrange the topping over the pancakes. Sprinkle with the coriander (cilantro) and serve at once.

CHAPTER 2

Vegetable Dishes

Stir-fry Cabbage and Ginger

Humble Savoy cabbage is transformed in seconds into a delectable but simple accompaniment to roasted or grilled (broiled) meats, game or poultry.

Serves 6–8

1 large Savoy cabbage
3 tablespoons of sunflower oil
2 tablespoons of mild chilli oil
8cm/3" ginger, peeled and grated

Salt and freshly ground black pepper
1 level tablespoon of (DF) margarine, or chilli oil for
    serving

Halve the cabbage, remove any hard white core/stem and slice very finely.
Heat the oils in a wok and fry the cabbage with the ginger, salt and pepper until just softened.
Serve hot with the margarine or chilli oil dotted all over it, and a little black pepper.

Exotic Pea Purée

An exotic version of the popular English dish, mushy peas, this is delicious with roast or grilled (broiled) fish, meat and poultry and its vivid colour brightens up the simplest lamb chop.

Serves 6–8

1kg/2.2lb/7 cups of frozen peas
1 large bunch of coriander (cilantro) or 3 x 15g/¹/₂oz
  supermarket packets, washed
Salt and freshly ground black pepper to taste
Grated nutmeg to taste

Dash of (GF) chilli sauce/oil
1 tablespoon (DF) margarine
200ml/7fl. oz/³/₄ cup of coconut cream

Cook the peas in salted boiling water until tender – about 3–5 minutes. Drain and process half of them in a food processor. Scrape the mixture into a bowl.

Trim the big bunch of coriander (cilantro), removing the stalks, and throw them away. (The supermarket packets are usually trimmed.)

Place the rest of the peas with the coriander (cilantro) and remaining ingredients in the food processor and process until smooth. Scrape this mixture into the first pea purée and blend together. Adjust the seasoning to taste. Transfer to a warm serving dish and cover until needed.

Nutty Vegetable Roulade

This enticing vegetarian dish is ideal for Christmas lunch. You can also change the filling from sweetcorn into a non-vegetarian left-over turkey recipe after Christmas.

Serves 6

FILLING

350g/12oz of parsnips, peeled and chopped
25g/1oz of (DF) margarine
2 tablespoons of soya cream
Freshly grated nutmeg
475g/16oz/2⅓ cups of whole sweetcorn drained

ROULADE

40g/1½oz of (DF) margarine
25g/1oz of rice flour
300ml/10fl. oz/1¼ cups of unsweetened soya milk
1 teaspoon of fresh thyme leaves
Salt and freshly ground black pepper
125g/4½oz/1 cup of grated courgette (zucchini)
100g/3½oz/¾ cup of chopped, toasted mixed nuts
3 large free-range eggs, separated
Cayenne pepper

Preheat the oven to 200°C/400°F/Gas mark 6.

Grease and line a large non-stick roulade tin with (DF) margarine and greaseproof (wax) paper. Next make the filling. Boil the parsnips until soft. Drain and then mash with the margarine, soya cream and nutmeg until smooth. Season to taste with salt and pepper. Stir in the sweetcorn, cover and keep warm.
Make the roulade by first melting the margarine. Beat in the flour and then incorporate the milk until you have a smooth sauce. Season to taste with thyme, salt and pepper. Then stir in the grated courgette (zucchini), half the mixed nuts and the egg yolks and remove from the heat.
In a large bowl, whisk up the egg whites until stiff and spoon one tablespoonful into the courgette (zucchini) mixture and blend gently. Now fold in the remaining egg whites very carefully with a metal spoon.
Scrape the mixture into the prepared tin and sprinkle with a little cayenne pepper.
Bake for 15–20 minutes until puffy but firm. Turn the roulade onto a piece of greaseproof (wax) paper that has been sprinkled with the remaining nuts.
Peel off the baking paper and throw away. Slice off both ends (if they look a little dry).
Spread the warm filling mixture over the roulade and gently use the paper underneath to help you roll up the roulade.
Slide the roulade carefully onto a warm serving dish and decorate with fresh parsley.
Accompany the dish with Cranberry Sauce (*see page 61*).

Honey Glazed Turnips

It's virtually impossible to get me to eat a turnip, but seduced by the idea of wild honey and thyme I succumbed to bribery. I now treat them with respectful awe that anything so bland can be transformed into something so delicious.

Serves 6–8

24 baby turnips, peeled and trimmed

2 heaped tablespoons of (GF/DF) four-grain
   mustard

6 tablespoons of runny honey

2 tablespoons of sunflower oil

Salt and freshly ground black pepper

2 heaped teaspoons of fresh thyme leaves

Preheat the oven to 180°C/350°F/Gas mark 4.

Add the turnips to a pan of boiling water. Return to the boil and cook for 5 minutes just to soften them. Drain and refresh under hot water and leave to dry out a bit.
Gently heat the mustard, honey and oil together and season with a little salt and pepper. Place the turnips on a non-stick baking sheet, pour the honey over them and sprinkle with thyme. Bake in the oven until golden brown and sticky, about 1³/₄ hours, or until cooked through, basting occasionally with the glaze so that they brown evenly.

Celeriac Dauphinoise

You can always replace half of the celeriac with potato slices if you find this recipe too expensive. It has a soft and delicious flavour and is ideal with grilled (broiled) fish, game and roasts of all sorts.

Serves 8

2 celeriac roots, peeled, quartered and very thinly
   sliced
1 large onion, peeled, halved and very finely sliced
Salt, freshly ground black pepper and nutmeg
(DF) margarine

1 plump clove of garlic, peeled and crushed
A few thyme leaves
300ml/10fl. oz/1¼ cups of made-up (GF) vegetable
   stock
Cayenne pepper

Set the oven to 180°C/350°F/Gas mark 4.

In an ovenproof dish, gradually layer the celeriac with the onion. Sprinkle salt, pepper and nutmeg over each layer, dotting with margarine, garlic and thyme leaves. Continue until all of the celeriac and onion have been used up.
Pour the stock over the top layer and finally sprinkle with cayenne pepper.
Bake in the oven until crispy on top and soft all the way through (about 2 hours). Check occasionally – if it looks as though it is starting to dry out add a little more stock.
Serve the Celeriac Dauphinoise piping hot.

Roast Squash, Chestnuts and Sweet Potatoes

This is a robust accompaniment to roast turkey, pheasant or grouse, especially at Christmas time. It is also unusual and delicious with roast pork or wild boar.

Serves 6–8

1 butternut squash, peeled, halved and seeded
1kg/2.2lb/7 cups of sweet (or normal) potatoes,
    peeled (1.5kg/3.3lb for 8 people or more)
200ml/7fl. oz/³/₄ cup of olive oil

Salt and freshly ground black pepper
A little sprinkling of grated cloves and nutmeg
12 whole cloves
240g/8oz/1 ¹/₂ cups of whole peeled chestnuts

Preheat the oven to 180°C/350°F/Gas mark 4.

Cut the squash and the potatoes into equal size pieces so that they will take a uniform time to cook. Bring a large pan of water to the boil and blanch the vegetables for 3 minutes in the boiling water. Refresh under cold water and leave to dry out for 10 minutes.
Brush the squash and potato pieces with oil and spread them evenly over an oiled baking sheet. Season with salt, pepper, grated cloves and nutmeg and then sprinkle with the whole cloves. Roast in the oven for about 1 ¹/₂ hours. Add the chestnuts 15 minutes before the end so that they heat through.
Serve straight from the oven and remind everyone not to eat the cloves!

Sweet Potato and Orange Purée

In order to be able to enjoy my own dinner parties, I usually prepare the vegetables in the morning and nuke them in the microwave as the meat is being carved. No steam, splashes or smells is the essence of a good dinner party in my tiny kitchen.

Serves 6–8

1.5kg/3.3lb/10½ cups of sweet potatoes, peeled and chopped

The grated rind and juice of 2 large oranges

Salt and freshly ground black pepper to taste

1 heaped tablespoon of (DF) margarine

Freshly grated nutmeg to taste

Remove any blemishes from the potatoes and then cook in boiling salted water for 20 minutes or until very soft. Turn off the heat and drain them. Return to the saucepan and mash the potatoes with all of the remaining ingredients until light and fluffy and without lumps. Transfer to a warm serving dish and keep warm until needed.

CHAPTER 3

Pizza, Pasta and Risotto

Chorizo and Artichoke Pizza

Intoxicating, hot and spicy; Spanish or Portuguese sausage is so versatile, eaten cold with a glass of chilled port, or sizzling on a pizza.

Serves 4

BASE
100g/3½oz/½ cup of rice flour
100g/3½oz/½ cup of potato flour
100g/3½oz/½ cup of maize flour
1 teaspoon of salt
5 tablespoons of olive oil
14g/½oz of easy-bake (instant) yeast
1 teaspoon of caster (superfine) sugar
200ml/7fl. oz/¾ cup of warm water

TOPPING
2 cloves of garlic, peeled and crushed
1 small red chilli, seeded and chopped
2 tablespoons of olive oil
425g/15oz/2 cups of canned chopped tomatoes,
    excess liquid drained off
2 tablespoons of tomato purée (paste)
A handful of fresh basil, shredded
Salt and freshly ground black pepper
150g/5oz/1⅓ cups of chorizo sausages, skinned and
    sliced
400g/14oz of canned artichoke hearts, drained and
    halved
A sprinkling of cayenne pepper
Grated sheep's, goat's or non-dairy cheese (optional)

Set the oven at 200°C/400°F/Gas mark 6.

Next, sieve and combine the flours, add the salt and 3 tablespoons of olive oil in a mixing bowl.
Add the yeast, sugar and water and stir until the ingredients come together.
Turn the dough onto a floured board and knead until smooth, adding more flour if necessary.
Clean the bowl and brush it with the remaining oil. Return the dough to the bowl and turn it so that it is completely covered in oil.
Cover with a cloth and leave to rise for 30 minutes.
Meanwhile, make the topping. First cook the garlic and chopped chilli in the oil for a second or two. Stir in the tomatoes and purée (paste), simmer for 5 minutes. Add the basil, salt and pepper.
Divide the dough into 2 or 4 flat circles. Oil a non-stick baking sheet and slide each pizza onto it. Flatten out each one and tidy the sides. Cover with the topping, then sprinkle with chorizo and the artichoke halves. Top the pizza with cheese, if using, and then sprinkle the cayenne over it and bake for about 10 minutes. Carefully slide the pizzas onto hot plates. Serve immediately.

Crab Cream Fettuccini

Fresh or frozen crab is always available in good supermarkets so you can serve this pasta any time of the year with a tossed green salad, or stir-fried sugar-snaps and dwarf (green) beans.

Serves 4

2 orange peppers, seeds and cores removed

375g/12$^{1}/_{2}$oz/4$^{1}/_{2}$ cups of corn and parsley (GF) fettuccini

1 tablespoon of olive oil

1 clove of garlic, peeled and chopped

1 bunch of spring/salad onions (scallions), trimmed and sliced

1 mild red chilli, seeded and chopped

2 stems of lemon grass, trimmed and finely chopped

454g/16oz /$^{2}/_{3}$ cup of fresh or frozen prepared crab meat

Salt and freshly ground black pepper

The juice of 1 lemon

200ml/7fl. oz/$^{3}/_{4}$ cup of coconut cream

Extra oil

1 tablespoon finely chopped coriander (cilantro) leaves

First, finely slice the peppers. Then cook the pasta following the packet's instructions in boiling salted water. Meanwhile heat the oil in a wok and stir-fry the peppers until golden-edged, then add the garlic, onions, chilli and lemon grass and cook for a couple of minutes. Stir in the crab meat and season with salt and pepper. Mix in the lemon juice and then the coconut cream. Bring to the boil and remove from the heat.

Drain and refresh the pasta under hot water and return to the pan. Toss in extra oil, salt and pepper.

Serve the pasta immediately on hot plates with the crab cream and sprinkle with coriander (cilantro) leaves.

Char-grilled Chicken Pasta With Pesto

Hopelessly addicted to fresh coriander (cilantro), I have deviously incorporated it into most of my favourite recipes. In this dish I have used it in place of the more traditional basil in the pesto sauce.

Serves 6

300ml/10fl. oz/1¼ cups of olive oil

3 fresh rosemary sprigs, halved

4 chicken breasts

500g/16½oz/6 cups of corn or rice (GF) pasta tubes

1 large bunch (60g/2oz/4 cups) of fresh coriander (cilantro)

30g/1oz of fresh parsley

1 clove of garlic, peeled and crushed

100g/3½oz/½ cup of pine nuts , ground in a food processor

Salt and freshly ground black pepper

Brush a char-grill pan with a little of the oil. Lay on the rosemary and chicken breasts and cook until the chicken is crispy and cooked through (about 10 minutes). Then slice diagonally into bite size pieces. Discard the rosemary.

Whilst the chicken is cooking, boil the pasta in a pan of salted water until just tender. Drain and refresh under hot water. Toss in a bowl with one tablespoon of the olive oil. Mix in the chicken pieces.

In a food processor, blend the remaining oil with the coriander (cilantro), parsley, garlic and pine nuts until smooth. Stir the coriander (cilantro) pesto sauce into the pasta, adjust the seasoning if necessary, and serve immediately.

Gnocchi with Walnut and Lemon Sauce

This was a fun and economical dish that we adored making in Lucca (Italy) when we were staying in the mountains last spring.

Serves 4 (or 6 as a starter)

SAUCE	GNOCCHI
3 large cloves of garlic, peeled and crushed	1kg/2.2lb/7 cups of floury potatoes
Chilli oil and extra virgin olive oil (according to taste)	1 large free-range egg
100g/3½oz/½ cup of finely chopped walnuts	200g/7oz/1½ cups of potato flour
Grated rind and juice of 3 large lemons	75g/3oz/⅓ cup of (DF) margarine
2 teaspoons of caster (superfine)sugar	15g/½oz/½ cup of chopped oregano leaves
Salt and freshly ground black pepper	Freshly ground black pepper
15g/½oz/¼ cup of chopped fresh parsley	
	Extra flour for dusting
	1 teaspoon of salt
	15g/½oz/½ cup of freshly shredded basil leaves

First make the sauce. Cook the garlic in olive oil mixed with the chilli oil (8 tablespoons for 4 people, or 12 tablespoons for 6 people) for a few seconds. Stir in the walnuts and lemon rind and cook for a few more seconds. Add the lemon juice and sugar, salt, pepper and parsley. Keep the sauce warm.

Now make the gnocchi. Peel the potatoes and boil until soft enough to mash. Drain and mash with all the gnocchi ingredients. Allow to cool.

Dust your hands with flour and shape the mixture into walnut size pieces. When the pieces are the correct shape and size, press the back of a fork a little way into the gnocchi to slightly indent and decorate.

Bring a very large pan of water to the boil with 1 teaspoon of salt and then drop the gnocchi into the water in batches and cook for just 30 seconds. Drain and keep warm in a serving dish.

Pour the sauce over the gnocchi. Serve piping hot, sprinkled with the shredded basil leaves.

Red Pepper Spaghetti

This is a great substitute for tomatoes, which I cannot eat because they are too acidic. Add minced meat or poultry for a great Bolognese sauce.

Serves 6

2 medium onions, peeled and finely chopped

2 tablespoons of olive oil

2 plump cloves of garlic, peeled and crushed

1 plump chilli, seeds removed

Plenty of fresh thyme leaves

4 big red peppers, stalks, pith and seeds removed

1 litre/32fl. oz/4 cups of carrot juice

Salt and freshly ground black pepper

600g/21oz/7 cups of (GF) spaghetti (corn, millet or rice only)

Extra olive oil

15g/¹/₂oz/¹/₂ cup of shredded basil leaves

Cook the onions gently in the oil for 5 minutes and then add the garlic. Chop up the chilli and stir it in with the thyme.

Now chop up the red peppers, add to the onions and cook for 10 minutes until browned in patches only.

Pour in the carrot juice, bring to the boil, then turn down the heat a little and simmer for 30 minutes. Season to taste with salt and pepper. Cool and liquidize.

Cook the spaghetti, following the instructions on the packet. Drain and toss in a little extra olive oil.

Serve immediately on a huge warm dish with the sauce poured over and shredded basil leaves sprinkled on top.

Red Wine Risotto

This dish, with its deep, rich Burgundy colours, is ideal for a winter lunch or supper with a full-bodied bottle of Italian red wine.

Serves 6

150g/5oz/1½ cups of (DF) margarine

2 large red onions, peeled and finely chopped

500g/16½oz/2½ cups of risotto rice

600ml/20fl. oz/2½ cups of Valpolicella or other fruity full-bodied red wine

Salt and freshly ground black pepper

1 tablespoon of (GF) vegetable stock powder

1 litre/1¾ pints/4 cups of boiling water

500g/16½oz of ready-cooked, peeled beetroots (beets)

3 tablespoons of chopped parsley.

Melt 100g/3½oz/1 cup of the margarine over a medium heat, add the onions and cook gently until nearly soft. Add the rice and stir for a minute. Pour in the red wine and season with salt and pepper. Simmer for 5 minutes.

Mix the stock powder into the water and pour into the rice. Simmer for 10 minutes.

Chop up the beetroots (beets) into bite size cubes and stir into the rice. Simmer for 10 more minutes and then fold in the remaining margarine. Adjust the seasoning to taste.

Serve on a large warm dish sprinkled with chopped parsley.

Spinach and Garlic Risotto

This is simplicity itself and is ideal for lunch, or as a starter. I frequently eat this dish with anchovies dotted all over the top, and a mixed salad.

Serves 6

4 tablespoons of olive oil

1 large onion, peeled and finely chopped

2 large cloves of garlic, peeled and crushed

250g/8½oz/1¼ cups of arborio rice

500g/17oz/9 cups of fresh or frozen (and defrosted) leaf spinach – do not use chopped spinach

300ml/10fl. oz/1¼ cups of dry white vermouth

Salt and freshly ground black pepper

800ml/28fl. oz/3½ cups of (GF) vegetable stock

The juice of 1 lemon

Grated nutmeg

1 tablespoon of fresh oregano leaves

½ tablespoon of (DF) margarine

Heat the oil and gently cook the onion until soft, but not brown.

Add the garlic. Cook for a moment and then stir in the rice and cook for a few minutes.

Mix in the spinach leaves followed by the vermouth. Season and then pour in the stock.

Bring to the boil and simmer for 35 minutes, or until the rice is swollen and soft (top up with water if necessary).

Stir in the lemon juice, nutmeg, oregano and margarine and serve very hot.

This is delicious with grated pecorino (romano) cheese on top.

CHAPTER 4

Fish and Seafood

Plaice in Tomato and Basil Hollandaise

Thick fillets of fish are successfully roasted in the oven at a very high temperature. This produces crispy skin and juicy flesh inside.

Serves 4

4 whole plaice, filleted into halves
Sunflower oil
Salt and freshly ground black pepper
1 tablespoon of dry white vermouth

TOMATO AND BASIL
HOLLANDAISE
175g/6oz/1⅓ cup of (DF) margarine
4 large free-range egg yolks
1 tablespoon of water
1 tablespoon of lemon juice
Salt and freshly ground black pepper
350g/12oz/2 cups of tomatoes, fresh or canned,
    skinned, drained and finely chopped
15g/½oz/½ cup of basil leaves, shredded

Extra basil leaves for decoration

Preheat the oven to 200°C/400°F/Gas mark 6.

Brush the plaice with a little oil, season and bake for about 5 minutes on a non-stick roasting tray with the vermouth sprinkled over.
Next, make the hollandaise sauce. Put the margarine into a saucepan and bring to the boil. Put the egg yolks, water, lemon juice, salt and pepper into a food processor and blend briefly.
As soon as the margarine comes to the boil, turn on the food processor and pour the margarine into the machine, continuing to blend until the sauce is thick. Turn off the processor and add the tomatoes and basil leaves. Adjust the seasoning if necessary. Pour the sauce into a bowl.
Serve the plaice on a warm plate with a pool of sauce and sprinkle with extra basil leaves.

Ocean Pie

This is all seafood and fish and omits the more traditional eggs, therefore is quicker to make and rather more French!

Serves 6–8

600ml/20fl. oz/2½ cups of ready-made (GF) fish
  stock

1 small red onion, peeled and finely chopped

½ a lemon

1 teaspoon of fresh thyme leaves

1 bay leaf

950g/2lb/5½ cups of cod fillet, skinned and boned

400g/14oz/3½ cups of frozen seafood, defrosted

200ml/7fl. oz/¾ cup of dry white vermouth

100g/3½oz/½ cup of (DF) margarine

50g/2oz/⅓ cup of rice flour

250ml/8fl. oz/1 cup of soya cream

Salt and freshly ground black pepper

15g/½oz/½ cup of fresh dill, chopped

1kg/2.2lb/7 cups of potatoes, peeled and trimmed

1 small whole celeriac, peeled and blemishes
  removed

Grated nutmeg

Extra margarine and some cayenne pepper

Set the oven to 200°C/400°F/Gas mark 6.

Place the stock in a pan and add the onion, lemon, thyme and bay leaf. Bring to the boil and cook for 10 minutes.

Chop the cod into bite size pieces. Reduce the heat, discard the lemon then add the cod and seafood.

Add the vermouth and poach gently for 3 minutes. Leave to cool away from the heat.

Melt half of the margarine in a large saucepan and beat in the flour. Gradually incorporate the vermouth stock.

Drain the fish, reserving the juices, then slowly beat the fish juices into the sauce until it is thick and smooth. Bring to the boil and cook for 1 minute, stirring all the time. Blend in the soya cream and seafood and season with salt, pepper and dill. Leave to one side.

Make the mash by chopping up the chunks of potato and celeriac in the food processor and then cook in salted boiling water until very soft. Drain and return to the pan with the remaining margarine and salt, pepper and nutmeg to taste and mash until smooth. Spoon the fish and sauce into a deep ovenproof dish and smooth the mash over it. Dot with a little extra margarine and a sprinkling of cayenne pepper and bake for 20 minutes. Serve straight from the oven.

Vodka Lime Seafood Salad

Beware of drinking and driving. The powerful kick this dish has could take you over the limit!
The vodka softens the fish, so it melts in your mouth.

Serves 4

600g/21oz/3½ cups of very fresh, or frozen, haddock
  fillets, skinned and boned
1 large mild red chilli, halved and seeded
½ a small red onion, peeled and finely chopped
170g/6oz/1½ cups of very fresh prawns (shrimp),
  shells removed
Salt and freshly ground black pepper

The juice of 1 large lemon
The grated rind and juice of 3 limes
4 tablespoons of vodka
2 tablespoons of chilli oil or olive oil
40g/1½oz of prepared lamb's lettuce (mâche)
A handful of coriander (cilantro) leaves to garnish

Cut the fish into attractive slender lengths and finely chop the chilli.

Mix the fish and chilli with the onion, prawns (shrimp), salt and pepper, lemon juice, rind and juice of the limes, vodka and chilli oil and leave to marinate for 2–4 hours, or overnight, in a shallow dish under clingfilm (plastic wrap).

Arrange the fish salad and all its juices on a serving plate with the lamb's lettuce (mâche) and sprinkle with a little chopped coriander (cilantro).

Alternatively, serve the salad on individual plates with slices of (GF) sourdough bread to mop up the juices.

Fresh Tuna and Quails' Egg Salad Niçoise

A perfect main course for the summer, easy to prepare and to transport outside with a couple of cool bottles of wine and fresh (GF) bread to mop up the dressing.

Serves 6 (or 12 as a starter)

1kg/2.2lb/7 cups of baby new potatoes, scrubbed

600g/21oz/7 cups of French dwarf (green) beans, topped and tailed

24 baby tomatoes, wiped and halved

1 small red onion, very finely sliced

24 black olives, stoned

3 tablespoons of chopped fresh parsley

Salt and freshly ground black pepper

24 quails' eggs, hard boiled for 3 minutes in boiling water, then transferred to cold water

12 anchovy fillets, drained and halved

3 tablespoons of virgin olive oil

2 tablespoons of lemon juice

1 large clove of garlic, peeled and crushed

6 large fresh tuna steaks or 12 small

Extra olive oil

Cook the potatoes in salted boiling water until just soft. Drain and put in a large dish.

Cook the beans, ensuring that they remain crunchy. Drain and refresh under cold water and mix with the potatoes.

Add in the tomatoes, onion, olives, half the parsley, salt and pepper. Peel and halve the eggs and mix into the salad. Add the anchovies.

Mix the oil, lemon juice and garlic together and sprinkle all over the salad.

Finally, brush the tuna fish with a little oil and grill (broil) or char-grill until just cooked through.

Place each steak on a bed of salad, sprinkle with the remaining parsley and serve or chill until needed.

For a more economical alternative, cook 540g/18oz of fresh tuna then flake the flesh into the salad.

Thai Coconut Sauté

More and more delicious Asian and Indian spice mixtures and ingredients are selling in supermarkets so that we can experiment with the flavours we so eagerly devour on holidays abroad.

Serves 2 (double the quantities to serve 4)

100g/3½oz of rice

16 x 6–7cm/2½ inch prawns (shrimp) in shells, peeled but tails left intact (or 200g/7oz/1¾ cups of peeled, defrosted prawns [shrimp])

1 large red pepper, trimmed and finely sliced

1 bunch of salad onions, trimmed and sliced

1 small mild red chilli, seeded and chopped

1 big clove of garlic, peeled and crushed

1 tablespoon each of sunflower oil and chilli oil

2–3 teaspoons of red Thai spice

285ml/10fl. oz/1¼ cups of coconut milk

Salt and freshly ground black pepper

The juice of 2 limes

1 tablespoon of fresh coriander (cilantro) leaves

Cook the rice in salted boiling water until tender.

Meanwhile slit the inside length of the prawns (shrimp) to prevent them curling up too much.

Drain and refresh the rice under hot water and keep warm.

Stir-fry the red pepper, onions, chilli and garlic in the oils in a heated wok over a high heat until softened but not browned. Stir in the red Thai spice and cook for a minute. Mix in the coconut milk and season with salt and pepper. Simmer for 1 minute with the lime juice.

Spoon the rice into the centre of two hot plates. Spoon over the prawns (shrimp) and sauce.

Sprinkle with coriander (cilantro) and serve.

SERVING SUGGESTION

Try serving with fragrant Thai rice.

Grilled Salmon on Puy Lentils

Well-produced farmed salmon is perfectly good but wild salmon is wonderful and as full of character as the fishermen who catch it.

Serves 4

2 tablespoons of chilli olive oil

1 tablespoon of fresh thyme leaves

1 large red onion, peeled and finely chopped

247g/8oz/1⅓ cups of canned puy lentils, drained (or 247g/8oz/1⅓ cups of dried puy lentils, cooked for 45 minutes instead of 8 minutes)

2 large cloves of garlic, peeled and crushed

Salt and freshly ground pepper

1 tablespoon of balsamic vinegar

300ml/10fl. oz/1¼ cups of water

3 tablespoons of chopped parsley

3 tablespoons of dry sherry

A little olive oil

4 x 200g/7oz salmon steaks

1 tablespoon of (DF) margarine

Add the chilli olive oil and thyme leaves to a frying pan and cook the onion gently until soft. Add the lentils, garlic, salt and pepper and lastly the vinegar. Simmer for 8 minutes, adding the water as soon as the mixture starts to stick. Stir in half the parsley and the sherry, adding more water if necessary.

In another pan fry the salmon steaks in a little olive oil until crispy on the outside and slightly underdone inside. Stir the margarine into the lentils.

Spoon a pool of lentils in juices onto each plate and serve with the salmon nesting on top. Sprinkle with the remaining parsley and enjoy it with a watercress salad or mashed potatoes.

Steamed Cod on Mint Purée

Cod is such an underrated fish and so I have decided to glamorize it to dinner party level!

Serves 4

1kg/2.2lb/8¾ cups of baby broad (fava) beans, defrosted
650g/23oz/4½ cups of potatoes, peeled and chopped
2 large free-range egg yolks
60g/2oz/¼ cup of (DF) margarine
750g/26oz fillet of fresh cod, skinned and boned
The juice of 1½ lemons

Salt and freshly ground black pepper
Freshly grated nutmeg
1 clove of garlic, peeled and crushed
2 tablespoons of soya cream
15g/½oz/½ cup of fresh mint leaves, finely chopped
A little olive oil and a few extra mint leaves
40g/1½oz/½ cup of fresh rocket (arugula) leaves

First, cook the broad (fava) beans in salted boiling water for 4 minutes. Drain and refresh under cold water.

Cook the potatoes in salted boiling water until soft. Meanwhile, peel all the skins off the broad (fava) beans and discard. Drain the potatoes and mash with the egg yolks and margarine until smooth.

Now steam or grill (broil) the cod, sprinkled with one third of the lemon juice, salt and pepper until it is just cooked through.

Purée the broad (fava) beans in a food processor with one third of the lemon juice, salt, pepper, nutmeg, garlic and soya cream. Beat this mixture into the mashed potatoes, adding the chopped mint. Adjust the seasoning. Divide the purée onto 4 warm plates. Put the cooked fish on top and sprinkle with the remaining lemon juice and the extra mint leaves to decorate.

Serve immediately, surrounded with rocket (arugula) leaves and drizzled with a little olive oil and black pepper.

Roast Swordfish with Basil

Swordfish has become very trendy and is now sold in most large supermarkets.

Serves 4

4 swordfish steaks, about 750g/26oz in weight
1 tablespoon of olive oil
Salt and freshly ground black pepper
400g/14oz/2 cups of butter (lima) beans, drained
2 tablespoons of chilli oil

1 large chilli, halved, trimmed, seeded and finely chopped
8 spring onions (scallions), trimmed and finely sliced
Lots of fresh basil, shredded
1 very large tomato, skinned, seeded and chopped

Preheat the oven to 200°C/400°F/Gas mark 6.

Brush the swordfish with the oil, salt and pepper and leave on a non-stick baking sheet for a moment. Cook the butter (lima) beans gently in the chilli oil with the chilli and spring onions (scallions) for 5 minutes.
Now put the fish in the oven. Add a little of the chopped basil to the beans, then add the chopped tomato and simmer for 5 minutes, by which time the fish will be cooked. Season the beans to taste.
Serve the fish steaks on hot plates with a large spoonful of beans sprinkled with the remaining fresh basil to decorate.

Smoked Haddock and Mushroom Roulade

This is a fun way of cooking haddock, which can be made into a party piece by using exotic wild mushrooms.

Serves 4–6

 *(Optional)*

350g/12oz of smoked haddock fillet, skinned and boned
300ml/10fl. oz/1¼ cups of soya milk
2 large bay leaves
125g/4oz/½ cup of (DF) margarine
25g/1oz of rice flour
2 teaspoons of mild (GF/DF) curry paste or powder
4 large free-range eggs, separated
Salt and freshly ground black pepper

3 tablespoons of grated pecorino (romano) or Etorki cheese (if sheep's cheese is tolerated), or 3 tablespoons chopped nuts, lightly browned in oven
Cayenne pepper
240g/8oz/3 cups of shiitake mushrooms, sliced
Grated nutmeg
6 tablespoons of soya cream

Set the oven at 200°C/400°F/Gas mark 6.

Line a roulade tin 25cm/10" x 36cm/14" with greased non-stick (wax) paper. Make sure the corners fit well and the paper reaches up each side.

Poach the haddock in the milk with the bay leaves, until just cooked. Flake it as soon as it is cooked. Discard the bay leaves and reserve the milk.

Make a roux with 50g/1¾oz of the margarine, melting it in a non-stick saucepan and gradually beating in the flour and curry paste. Beat in the reserved milk and cook until smooth and thick. Cool and beat in the fish and egg yolks. Season to taste with salt and pepper.

In another bowl, whisk the egg whites until stiff. Fold 1 spoonful into the fish and then gently fold the rest in with a metal spoon. Tip and scrape this into the tin and bake for 15–20 minutes until firm.

Cool for a few minutes and then tip onto a large piece of greaseproof (wax) paper that has been scattered with sheep's cheese, nuts or just a little cayenne pepper. Peel away the paper from the roulade and discard. Slice off both ends of the roulade if they are a little dry. Cover with a clean tea towel.

Now melt the remaining margarine and cook the mushrooms for a few minutes. Season with salt, pepper and nutmeg. Stir in the cream and remove from the heat. Remove the cloth and lift the roulade onto a warm serving dish. Spread the mushroom filling all over it and, using the paper underneath to help you, roll up the roulade. Finally, just pull off the paper and discard. Serve immediately with a green salad.

Quick Salmon Soufflé

Soufflés are cheap and easy – ideal for supper with a salad or as an enterprising starter.

Serves 3

(DF) margarine, for greasing
2 tablespoons of (GF) breadcrumbs
200g/7oz of fresh salmon fillets
1 tablespoon of very dry white vermouth
Salt and freshly ground black pepper
1 heaped tablespoon of (DF) margarine
2 heaped tablespoons of rice flour

3 tablespoons of soya cream
3 large free-range egg yolks, beaten together in a
    bowl
Grated nutmeg
5 egg whites
Cayenne pepper

Preheat the oven to 200°C/400°F/Gas mark 6.

Grease the inside of a large soufflé dish with just enough margarine and coat all over with breadcrumbs.

Poach the salmon in a little water with the vermouth, salt and freshly ground black pepper until just cooked through. Cool, then remove the skin and bones and flake the fish, reserving the poaching liquid.

Melt the margarine in a non-stick saucepan and beat in the flour. Add the poaching liquid and then the salmon.

Beat until smooth and thick. Bring to the boil and cook for 1 minute. Remove from the heat. Add the soya cream and egg yolks and mix well. Season with pepper and nutmeg and blend briefly in the food processor until pale pink and smooth. Transfer to a bowl.

In a clean bowl, stiffly whisk the eggs with a pinch of salt until firm. Stir one spoonful into the salmon and then quickly and gently fold the rest in with a metal spoon. Spoon into the prepared dish and sprinkle with cayenne pepper.

Bake for 30–35 minutes until golden, firm and well risen. Serve immediately.

Tuna Fishcakes and Dill Sauce

Corn meal is a brilliant substitute for flour, which is not tolerated by coeliacs, and should satisfy even the most discerning palate.

Serves 6

15g/¹/₂oz/¹/₂ cup of fresh dill, chopped

1 tablespoon of mild (GF) mustard

4 tablespoons of (DF/GF) mayonnaise

3 tablespoons of soya cream

1 tablespoon of olive oil

400g/14oz/2¹/₂ cups of tuna fish in brine, drained

900g/32oz/6 cups of potatoes, peeled, boiled and mashed

Freshly grated nutmeg

Salt and freshly ground black pepper

A dash of (GF) Tabasco sauce/hot chilli oil

1 tablespoon of chopped fresh parsley

1 tablespoon of (DF) margarine

(GF) cornflour (cornstarch) for dusting

2 eggs, beaten

200g/7oz/1¹/₂ cups of fine corn meal

Oil for frying

First, make the sauce by mixing the dill, mustard, mayonnaise, cream and oil. Season to taste, then cover, and chill until needed.

Mash the tuna fish with the potatoes and season with nutmeg, salt and pepper, Tabasco sauce and parsley, then beat in the margarine.

Dust your clean hands with cornflour (cornstarch) and roll the mixture into 12 patties. Dip each fishcake into the beaten egg and roll in corn meal. Chill in the deep freeze for half an hour. Now fry in a little hot oil until crispy and golden, about 5 minutes on each side. Drain briefly onto absorbent paper and serve immediately with the dill sauce.

CHAPTER 5

Meat Dishes

Steak and Kidney Pudding

Traditional English pub food at its best. The pudding is packed with spices and herbs, so the aroma when it is cut open is wonderful.

Serves 5

FILLING

560g/20oz/2½ cups of chuck steak, trimmed and chopped

275g/10oz/1¼ cups of kidneys of your choice, trimmed and chopped

4 level tablespoons of well seasoned (GF) flour

2 tablespoons of olive oil

1 medium onion, peeled and sliced finely

200ml/7fl. oz/¾ cup of dry sherry

1 level tablespoon of (GF) Dijon mustard

1 tablespoon of (GF) Worcestershire sauce

A few drops of (GF) Tabasco sauce

1 teaspoon of mixed (pie) spice or allspice

3 cloves, and a pinch of grated nutmeg

SUET PASTRY

100g/3½oz/¾ cup of rice flour

100g/3½oz/¾ cup of buckwheat flour

75g/2½oz/½ cup of potato flour

3 teaspoons of (GF) baking powder

150g/5oz/1 cup of (GF) shredded suet

Salt and freshly ground black pepper

250ml/8fl. oz/1 cup of water

1.7 litre/3 pint pudding bowl

Make the filling first. Toss the steak and kidneys in the flour. Heat the oil in a large pan and cook the onion first for 5 minutes until soft, but not brown. Add the meat and seal on all sides. Pour in the sherry, stir in the mustard and Worcestershire sauce, Tabasco sauce, spice, cloves and nutmeg and simmer gently while you make the pastry.

Sift and mix the flours with the baking powder. Fold in the suet, salt and pepper. Now gradually mix in the cold water using a couple of blunt edged knives. The dough will slowly come together and you will need to use your hands to form the dough into a ball and knead briefly.

Roll out three quarters of the pastry on a floured board into a 35cm/14" circle and then line an oiled pudding bowl with it. Quickly pour in the meat filling and then roll out the remaining pastry to cover the top. Seal by pinching the edges with cold water on your finger tips. Pierce the top with a sharp knife.

Cover the top of the pudding with greaseproof (wax) paper, making a central pleat by folding it over with plenty of space for the pastry to expand, and tie up with string. Place the bowl on a folded piece of foil in a large saucepan and fill with boiling water to half way up the bowl. Cover the saucepan with a lid or tightly wrapped foil and boil for 2 hours (checking the water level regularly) until the pastry is cooked and the meat is tender.

Lift the pudding bowl out of the saucepan and leave for 5 minutes. Remove the lid and serve the pudding in the bowl, wrapped in a clean white linen napkin.

Beef en Croûte with Tomato and Basil Hollandaise

This recipe can also be made with salmon, lamb, pork or veal. After Christmas, it's a good way of using up leftover turkey breast.

Serves 4 or

PASTRY

250g/9oz/1¾ cups of *The Stamp Collection* wheat free flour or ⅓ each of (GF) rice flour, maize flour and potato flour

A good pinch of salt

75g/2½oz/⅓ cup of (DF) margarine

75g/2½oz/⅓ cup of lard

1 large free-range egg yolk

4 tablespoons of cold water

BEEF FILLING

400g/14oz/3½ cups of button mushrooms, wiped and trimmed of stalks

2 tablespoons of olive oil

1 clove of garlic, peeled and chopped

2 teaspoons of fresh thyme leaves

Salt and freshly ground black pepper

725g/25oz of fillet steak, trimmed

Oil for brushing

½ a beaten egg

TOMATO AND BASIL HOLLANDAISE

350g/12oz/2 cups of tomatoes, fresh or canned, skinned, drained and finely chopped

175g/6oz/¾ cup of (DF) margarine

4 large free-range egg yolks

1 tablespoon of water

1 tablespoon of lemon juice

Salt and freshly ground black pepper

15g/½oz/½ cup of basil leaves, shredded

Set the oven to 200°C/400°F/Gas mark 6.

First, make the pastry. Put the flour into a large bowl and mix in the salt. Add the margarine and lard in pieces and mix with two blunt-edged knives, using one in each hand. Then rub the mixture with your clean finger tips, lifting and crumbling to aerate it. Make a well in the centre, add the egg and water and blend together. Work lightly and wrap in clingfilm (plastic wrap). Chill for 30 minutes.

Fill a bowl with boiling water and immerse the tomatoes for the sauce. Pierce the skin once or twice and leave for 3 minutes, then drain. Now peel off the skin, remove the seeds and chop up the flesh.

Finely slice the mushrooms and cook gently in the 2 tablespoons of oil, garlic and half the thyme. Season to taste and keep to one side.

Brush the beef with oil, season with salt, pepper and the remaining thyme. Divide the dough in half. Sprinkle flour on a board and roll the pastry into a rectangle, and trim with a sharp knife to about 2cm/³/₄" larger than the beef. Put half the mushrooms in the centre of the pastry and cover with the beef.

Spoon the remaining mushrooms over the top of the meat. Roll out the other half of the pastry and place over the beef, with a similar overhang of about 2cm/³/₄". Bring both pieces of pastry together and seal by pinching with your fingertips. Decorate with a few cut-out pastry leaves or flowers according to your artistic talents! Brush with beaten egg.

Very gently criss-cross the pastry with a blunt-edged knife and make a little incision in the centre to let the air escape. Bake in the oven for 35 minutes until golden.

While this is baking, make the Hollandaise sauce. Put the margarine into a saucepan and bring to the boil. Meanwhile put the egg yolks, water, lemon juice, salt and pepper into a food processor and blend briefly.

As soon as the margarine comes to the boil, turn on the food processor and pour the margarine into the machine. Continue to blend until the sauce is thick. Turn off the processor and add the tomatoes and basil leaves. Transfer the sauce to a warm serving bowl.

Carve the fillet into thick slices and serve with a pool of sauce. Crunchy broccoli and French beans balance the dish very nicely.

Lamb Fillet with Black Bean Salsa

I have used this recipe for black bean salsa with several other dishes, as familiarity makes for speed and ease in the kitchen.

Serves 6

---

1 × quantity of Black Bean Salsa (see *page 74*)
4 large boneless lamb neck fillets, trimmed
Chilli olive oil

Salt and freshly ground black pepper
1 tablespoon of fresh coriander (cilantro) leaves

First make the salsa and chill until needed.

When you are nearly ready to serve the meat, brush the lamb with a little chilli olive oil and season with salt and pepper. Grill (broil) or fry until crispy on the outside and pink inside (or according to taste), about 5–7 minutes on each side.

Carve the meat, arrange the slices on warm plates with a spoonful of the salsa beside it and decorate with a few coriander (cilantro) leaves.

Serve the remaining salsa separately.

Delicious with new potatoes and a green salad.

Lamb Dauphinoise

A layer of browned, sliced celeriac tops this mince and transforms it into easy, flexible party food. You can use any kind of mince: turkey, venison or veal are the less fattening options.

Serves 6

SAUCE
400g/14oz/1¾ cups of Greek-style set sheep's
  yoghurt or (DF) tofu dip, or (DF) soya yoghurt
4 tablespoons of freshly chopped coriander
  (cilantro) and mint leaves
1 small red chilli, halved, seeded and finely chopped
Salt and freshly ground black pepper

LAMB DAUPHINOISE
750g/26oz/3⅓ cups of best lean minced lamb

4 plump cloves of garlic, peeled and crushed
1 medium onion, peeled and chopped
Salt, freshly ground black pepper and grated nutmeg
1 tablespoon of dried mixed herbs
1 tablespoon of tomato purée (paste)
300ml/10fl. oz/1¼ cups of red wine
1 level tablespoon (GF) cornflour (cornstarch)
1 large or 2 small celeriac, peeled
25g/1oz of (DF) margarine
Cayenne pepper

Preheat the oven to 200°C/400°F/Gas mark 6.

First make the sauce. Mix all of the ingredients together, cover and chill until needed.
Cook the mince for a few minutes in a large pan over a low heat until it is evenly browned. Stir occasionally and do not allow it to stick.
Add three quarters of the garlic and the onion and cook for a further 2 minutes, stirring all the time. Add the seasoning, mixed herbs and tomato purée (paste). Then mix in the wine and simmer for 3 minutes.
Blend the cornflour (cornstarch) with 300ml/10fl. oz/1¼ cups of cold water in a mug until it is smooth. Stir the mixture into the lamb. Now bring the mince to the boil so that it thickens. Transfer this to a deep heatproof baking dish.
Remove any blemishes from the celeriac and chop it into thin and even slices, so it looks like potato slices. Have a saucepan of boiling water ready and blanch the prepared celeriac for 5 minutes. Drain and refresh under cold water.
Arrange a layer of celeriac over the mince, dot with margarine, the remaining garlic, salt and pepper. Cover with another layer of celeriac until it is all used up.
Sprinkle the top with a little cayenne pepper and dot with more margarine.
Bake until the celeriac is soft and cooked through, and the top is golden brown, about 45 minutes.
Now reduce the heat to 180°C/350°F/Gas mark 4 and cook for another 40 minutes.
Serve hot with a dollop of the sauce on the celeriac. Ideal with a green or mixed salad.

Orange Stuffed Lamb

Keep the lamb bones to make stock if you have time. Cool and refrigerate the drained stock, skim off the set fat and discard. Use the fresh stock in your recipe.

Serves 8

Thickly grated rind and juice of 1 large orange

1 level tablespoon of fresh chopped mixed herbs

2 plump cloves of garlic, peeled and crushed

300ml/10fl. oz/1¼ cups of water and white wine, mixed

2225g/4lb 12oz of leg lamb (weighed with bone and then boned and butterflied by your butcher)

Grated rind of 1 orange

15g/½oz of (DF) margarine

90g/3oz/1½ cups of 100% (WF) rye breadcrumbs

300ml/10fl. oz/1¼ cups of (WF) lamb stock

100g/3½oz/½ cup of dried apricots, finely chopped

30g/1oz of pine nuts

1 large orange, segmented and chopped

3 heaped tablespoons of finely chopped fresh parsley

Sea salt and freshly ground black pepper

1 heaped tablespoon of (GF) cornflour (cornstarch), mixed with a little cold water

---

Preheat the oven to 190°/375°F/Gas mark 5.

Put the grated orange rind and juice in a roasting tin with half the mixed herbs and one of the cloves of crushed garlic.

Pour over the water and wine mixture.

Next stuff the lamb. You need to mix in a bowl the grated rind of 1 orange, the remaining herbs and crushed garlic, mash in the margarine, breadcrumbs, 3 tablespoons of stock, apricots, nuts, chopped orange, parsley and seasoning.

Fill the lamb cavity with this mixture and then tie up at 25mm/1" intervals, using a skewer to fasten the end and keep in the stuffing.

Place in the pan and pour over all the remaining stock. Roast for 1½ hours, until crispy on the outside and pink inside. Leave to sit for 10 minutes before transferring to a carving board.

Make the gravy by boiling up the juices in the pan and scraping them around. Stir in the cornflour (cornstarch) and bring to the boil until thick and clear. Serve with the carved lamb.

Beef Casserole with Dumplings

Use a rich, fruity red wine like Barolo from Italy and the casserole will be meltingly tender and full of flavour.

Serves 6

BEEF CASSEROLE

1kg/2.2lb of stewing steak

2 tablespoons of seasoned (GF) cornflour (cornstarch)

2 tablespoons of olive oil

30g/1oz of (DF) margarine

1 large onion, sliced

125g/4½oz/⅔ cup of unsmoked streaky bacon, cut into strips

1 large carrot, finely chopped

2 stalks of celery, finely chopped

3 tablespoons of fresh chopped parsley

12 sage leaves, chopped

2 bay leaves

1 sprig of rosemary

3 cloves of garlic, peeled and crushed

Freshly grated nutmeg

Salt and freshly ground black pepper

1 bottle of Barolo, or a full-bodied red wine

225g/8oz/2½ cups of mushrooms of any kind, in quarters or halves, according to size

DUMPLINGS

50g/2oz/⅓ cup of buckwheat flour

50g/2oz/⅓ cup of rice flour

75g/2½oz/½ cup of potato flour

2 heaped teaspoons of (GF) baking powder

Salt and freshly ground black pepper

3 tablespoons of chopped parsley

75g/2½oz/½ cup of (GF) shredded suet

Set the oven at 150°C/300°F/Gas mark 2.

Cut the steak into bite size pieces and coat in the seasoned flour. Fry in the oil and margarine in a casserole dish until lightly browned.

Add the onion and bacon and fry for a further couple of minutes. Stir in the carrot, celery, all the herbs, garlic and seasoning.

Mix in the red wine and cover. Transfer to the oven and simmer for 2 hours.

Add the mushrooms and cook for the last 15 minutes.

While the casserole is cooking, make the dumplings. First, mix the flours and baking powder, salt and pepper and parsley together in a bowl.

Blend in the suet, but do not rub it in. Add just enough cold water to make a dough. Knead very lightly and shape into 12 dumplings. Place them all over the surface of the casserole and bake without the lid for the last half hour, until they are golden and crusty.

Serve piping hot with Celeriac Dauphinoise (*see page 24*)

Pork Chops with Lemon and Walnut Fettuccini

The lemon juice cuts through the richness of the pork making it a light meal. You can cook veal escalopes for an even lighter dish.

Serves 4

6–12 pork chops, trimmed of fat and boned
1 tablespoon of chilli olive oil
Salt and freshly ground black pepper
12 fresh sage leaves
2 plump cloves of garlic, peeled and crushed
1 teaspoon of ground cloves
500g/16½oz/6 cups of corn and parsley (GF)
   fettuccini

Extra oil (either sunflower, olive or chilli oil)
200ml/7fl. oz/¾ cup of white wine
The juice of 6 lemons
The grated rind of 2 lemons
100g/3½oz/1 cup of chopped walnuts
2 tablespoons of finely chopped parsley

Using a large pan, fry the chops over a medium heat in the chilli olive oil, seasoning them with salt, pepper and sage leaves.
Turn them over, add the garlic and cloves, reduce the heat and simmer until cooked through.
Cook the pasta in salted, boiling water in a large saucepan. Drain and refresh under hot water.
Return to the pan and toss in the extra oil of your choice and cover.
Add the wine and then the lemon juice, rind, and the walnuts to the pork chops and adjust the seasoning to taste. Simmer for 1 minute.
Serve the pasta in a large shallow dish and arrange the chops over it.
Spoon over all the sauce, sprinkle with parsley and serve immediately.

CHAPTER 6

Poultry and Game

Chicken in Walnut and Garlic Sauce

European walnuts are sweeter and milder than Californian nuts, and are very compatible with pasta or as an extra source of protein. This easy and unusual dish can be served with rice and a salad that can be prepared well in advance.

Serves 8

8 large chicken breasts, off the bone
12 tablespoons of olive oil
6 heaped tablespoons of roughly chopped walnuts

6 heaped tablespoons of chopped parsley
6 plump cloves of garlic, peeled and crushed
Plenty of salt and freshly ground black pepper

Set the oven to 200°C/400°F/Gas mark 6.

Place the chicken breasts in an ovenproof serving dish.
Put all the remaining ingredients into a food processor and whiz briefly into a sauce.
Spread the mixture over the chicken and bake in the oven for 40 minutes until golden.
Serve hot with potatoes, rice, pasta or bread to soak up all the lovely juices.

Baked Chicken and Spinach Crumble

A cheap and cheerful kitchen lunch or supper party, ideal for both children and adults. Perfect with baked potatoes.

Serves 6

6 chicken leg/thigh pieces, or 1 whole chicken cut into 6 portions
1 level tablespoon of (GF) vegetable bouillon powder in 500ml/16fl. oz/2 cups of water
1 sprig of rosemary
1 bay leaf
1 plump clove of garlic, peeled and crushed
Salt and freshly ground black pepper and grated nutmeg
4 thick slices of 100% pure rye-bread, processed into breadcrumbs

3 heaped tablespoons of oats
1 tablespoon of fresh thyme leaves
500g/17oz/9 cups of frozen leaf spinach, defrosted
1 heaped tablespoon of (DF) margarine plus 1 heaped teaspoon
2 tablespoons of (GF) cornflour (cornstarch)
250ml/8fl. oz/1 cup of soya cream
A little cayenne pepper
Sunflower oil

Preheat the oven to 200°C/400°F/Gas mark 6.

Cook the chicken pieces in a deep ovenproof dish in the stock and water with the rosemary, bay leaf, garlic, salt, pepper and nutmeg until tender (about 40 minutes). Cover with foil to keep the meat moist.

Meanwhile, mix the breadcrumbs, oats and thyme together with just a little salt, pepper and nutmeg. Cook the spinach for a few minutes in boiling water and drain. Dot with margarine and season to taste with a little salt, pepper and nutmeg and keep covered.

Drain all the juices from the chicken dish into a bowl and arrange the chicken neatly again. Make a white sauce in a saucepan by melting 1 heaped tablespoon of margarine and stirring in the cornflour (cornstarch). Gradually incorporate all the stock and juices until you have a thick smooth sauce. Stir in the soya cream and adjust seasoning.

Spoon this sauce all over the chicken and then cover with spinach and top with all the crumble mixture. Sprinkle with a little cayenne pepper and sunflower oil and bake for 30 minutes until golden and bubbling.

Prune and Walnut Stuffed Roast Chicken

A wonderful wintery combination also delicious stuffed into pheasant or turkey.

Serves 6

1 medium onion, finely chopped

2 tablespoons of olive oil

1 plump clove of garlic, peeled and crushed

50g/2oz/½ cup of walnut pieces, finely chopped

250g/9oz/1¼ cups of chopped, ready-to-eat stoned prunes

Salt and freshly ground black pepper

½ teaspoon of mixed (pie) spice

2 tablespoons of dry sherry

1 beaten egg

50g/2oz/1¾ cups of ground almonds

2 bay leaves

1.9 kg/4.2lb large free-range roasting chicken

9 rashers of rindless streaky bacon

4 sprigs of thyme

200ml/7fl. oz/¾ cup of dry cider

½ a (GF) chicken stock cube dissolved in 200ml/ 7fl. oz/¾ cup of boiling water

1 tablespoon of (GF) cornflour (cornstarch), dissolved in 1 tablespoon of cold water

2 tablespoons of chopped fresh parsley

In a non-stick pan, fry the onion in the oil until soft, for about 5 minutes, then add the garlic, walnuts, prunes, salt, pepper and mixed (pie) spice.

Cook for a couple of minutes and then add the sherry. As soon as it has evaporated, remove the saucepan from the heat and stir in the beaten egg and ground almonds.

Grease a large ovenproof dish with a little oil. Lay a bay leaf at each end.

Remove the fat pockets from the inside of the chicken and then slide a sharp knife under the breast skin and all over the meat. This is where you will put the stuffing. Insert a level tablespoon of stuffing into this area and pack the skin down into a good shape.

Now wrap the bacon strips around the chicken breast and squeeze gently into a neat packet. Place in the dish on the bay leaves and sprinkle with the thyme and more salt and pepper.

Mix the cider with the stock and water mixture and pour around the chicken. Bake for 1–1¼ hours until the bacon is crispy and the chicken has cooked through (if the bacon gets too crispy, cover it loosely with foil). The chicken is ready when the juices run clear when tested with a skewer.

Remove the chicken onto a warm plate whilst you transfer the juices to a small saucepan. Stir in the cornflour (cornstarch) and bring to the boil until cooked, thickened and clear again.

Serve slices of chicken on a warm plate with a pool of sauce and sprinkle over a little chopped fresh parsley.

Chestnut Stuffed Turkey with Bread Sauce and Cranberry Sauce

Christmas is always a difficult time for people with allergies, so there are plenty of Christmas and New Year recipes for everyone to enjoy. Buy (GF) sausages in advance and freeze them so that you can have them with traditional bacon rolls.

Serves 6–8

4kg/8.8lb large free-range turkey and giblets
1 onion, peeled and sliced
Plenty of fresh thyme and 3 bay leaves
2 whole cloves
Salt and freshly ground black pepper

STUFFING
450g/16oz/4 cups of raw (GF) sausage meat
420g/15oz/2 cups of chickpeas (garbanzo beans)
175ml/6fl. oz/³/₄ cup of sunflower oil
6 tablespoons of dry sherry
240g/8oz/1¹/₂ cups of prepared whole chestnuts, roughly chopped
Grated nutmeg
1 heaped teaspoon of allspice
1 heaped teaspoon of mixed (pie) spice
125g/4¹/₂oz/1 cup of luxury dried mixed fruit
1 large free-range egg, beaten
8 slices of smoked streaky bacon

200ml/7fl. oz/³/₄ cup of dry white wine or unsweetened apple juice
Oil for brushing
1 tablespoon of (GF) cornflour (cornstarch) dissolved in 2 tablespoons of water

BREAD SAUCE
100g/3¹/₂oz/²/₃ cup of flaked or ground white rice
200ml/7fl. oz/³/₄ cup of coconut milk
200ml/7fl. oz/³/₄ cup of soya cream
1 heaped teaspoon of (DF) margarine

CRANBERRY SAUCE
680g/24oz of fresh or frozen cranberries
The grated rind and juice of 2 oranges
4 tablespoons of sugar
A little (GF) cornflour (cornstarch) and cold water, mixed (optional)

Preheat the oven to 190°C/375°F/Gas mark 5.

Pull out any fat from inside the turkey and throw it away.
Put the giblets with half the onion, some thyme, 1 bay leaf, 2 cloves, salt and pepper in a deep pan and cover with 2 litres/3¹/₄ pints/2 quarts of water. Bring to the boil, then simmer for 2 hours until you have a good stock, topping up with water half way through if necessary (to make sure you end up with 1 litre/1³/₄ pints/4 cups). Drain the stock into a bowl and keep cool until needed. Next prepare the stuffing. Mix the sausage meat and chickpeas (garbanzo beans), oil and sherry in the food processor and process until smooth. Scrape this mixture into a big bowl and mix in the chestnuts, which will break them up a little more and then add salt and pepper. Add some

grated nutmeg, allspice, mixed (pie) spice and fresh thyme to taste. Then add the dried fruit and the beaten egg and mix well.

Carefully lift the skin up from the whole turkey breast and bone with a sharp knife, taking care not to break the skin. Carefully push the stuffing up under the skin as far as you can until it is packed full. Shape it roundly with your clean hands and then wrap up in bacon.

Put the turkey in a roasting tin on a bed of the remaining onion, bay leaves, some thyme, salt, pepper and wine or juice. Then brush the turkey all over with oil and a little more salt, pepper and thyme.

Cover with foil and roast the turkey for 2 hours, topping up the liquid level with stock. Remove the foil from the turkey and roast for another 30 minutes until golden. When the legs are pierced, the juices should run clear. Let the turkey sit for 15 minutes before carving.

During this time make the gravy by draining off all the juices into a pan (discarding the onions and bay leaves), and removing the excess fat with a spoon.

Add enough of the remaining stock to make lots of gravy. Stir in the cornflour (cornstarch) dissolved in cold water. Bring to the boil and cook for a few minutes. Adjust the seasoning and transfer to sauce boats.

To make the bread sauce, put the rice, coconut milk, salt, pepper and freshly grated nutmeg into a non-stick saucepan and simmer until soft and creamy. Add the soya cream and margarine, and keep warm until needed.

To make the cranberry sauce mix all of the ingredients and simmer for 10 minutes until the cranberries have burst and are soft and pulping. If the sauce is too runny stir in extra cornflour (cornstarch) and water mixed together and bring to the boil until it is clear and thick.

SERVING SUGGESTION

Serve with sausages, bacon rolls, roast potatoes, Brussels sprouts and chestnuts.

Turkey Breasts in Sage and Polenta Crumbs

I use lots of turkey now that it is so easy to buy ready-sliced into escalopes.

Serves 4

---

4 thick turkey escalopes, trimmed of all fat

4 thick slices of hard goat's or sheep's cheese

20 large sage leaves

6 slices of Parma ham (prosciutto), fat trimmed off

2 tablespoons of rice flour

Salt and freshly ground black pepper

2 eggs, beaten

4 tablespoons of polenta (maize) crumbs

Sunflower oil, to fry

Slice each escalope in half horizontally and lay out open. Place a slice of cheese and 3 sage leaves in each escalope and wrap 1½ pieces of Parma ham (prosciutto) around each fillet (to secure).

Season the flour with salt and pepper and then dust each escalope with it. Dip the escalopes in the beaten eggs and then roll in a plate of polenta crumbs. Heat the oil in a frying pan (skillet), add the remaining sage and fry the escalopes on each side for 5–6 minutes until crispy golden brown and cooked through. Drain on absorbent paper and serve immediately with new potatoes and salad.

Venison Loaf and Red Pepper Sauce

This is brilliant for a picnic as well as for a kitchen supper. (GF) breads, salad and a good (GF) chutney are all that is needed.

Serves 5

2 tablespoons of olive oil
1 medium onion, peeled and finely chopped
450g/16oz/2 cups of raw minced venison
450g/16oz/2 cups of raw (GF) sausage meat
1 tablespoon of chopped fresh tarragon leaves
1 teaspoon of fresh parsley leaves
2 plump cloves of garlic, peeled and crushed
Salt, pepper and grated nutmeg
1 teaspoon of allspice
1 large free-range egg, beaten
1 tablespoon of (GF) Worcestershire sauce
A little (GF) chilli sauce/oil

SAUCE

1 medium onion, peeled and chopped
1 tablespoon of olive oil
2 large red peppers, seeded, trimmed and chopped
2 cloves of garlic, peeled and crushed
2 chillies, seeded and chopped
1 teaspoon of thyme leaves
500ml/16fl. oz/2 cups of carrot juice
Salt and freshly ground black pepper

A non-stick metal terrine/loaf tin

Set the oven to 200°C/400°F/Gas mark 6.

Heat the oil in a pan and cook the onion until soft but not brown, for about 10 minutes. Put it into a large bowl and mix in all of the remaining ingredients.
Fill the tin with the venison mixture. Pat down firmly, cover with foil brushed with oil and bake in a shallow tray of water for 1 hour or until the juices run clear when a skewer is inserted.
Leave for 15 minutes before turning out onto a serving plate, either to eat hot with the sauce or cover and chill until needed.
To make the sauce, cook the onion in the oil with the peppers, garlic, chillies and thyme for 5 minutes over a medium heat. Add the carrot juice and season. Cook for 25 minutes over a high heat. Allow to cool and then liquidize. Adjust the seasoning and reheat to serve with the venison loaf.

Venison and Pickled Walnut Casserole

I always imagined that pickled walnuts were sweet and boozy, so I was very surprised when I was actually brave enough to taste one and discovered it wasn't remotely how I imagined, and rather delicious in this recipe.

Serves 6–8

2 tablespoons of olive oil

3 medium onions, peeled and finely sliced

1225g/2lb 11oz/5½ cups of stewing venison cubes

125g/4½oz/¾ cup of streaky bacon with rinds removed, chopped

2 heaped tablespoons of brown sugar

2 cloves of garlic, peeled and crushed

1 bay leaf

A small bunch of fresh thyme

2 sprigs of rosemary, leaves only

1 tablespoon of (GF) Worcestershire sauce

2 heaped tablespoons of tomato purée (paste)

Salt and freshly ground black pepper to taste

½ litre/16fl. oz/2 cups of red wine

790g/27oz/9 cups of pickled walnuts in malt vinegar

2 tablespoons of (GF) cornflour (cornstarch), dissolved in 3 tablespoons of cold water

25g/1oz of (DF) margarine

Set the oven to 180°C/350°F/Gas mark 4.

Put the oil in a casserole dish and slowly cook the onions for 8 minutes on the stove top. Then turn up the heat and sauté the venison cubes with the onions for a further 8 minutes. Now stir in the bacon, sugar, garlic, herbs, Worcestershire sauce, tomato purée (paste), salt and pepper. Pour in the wine and cover. Leave to simmer for 35 minutes.

Halve the walnuts before adding them with a tablespoon of the vinegar. (Throw out the remainder of the vinegar).

Transfer the venison casserole to the hot oven and cook for 1 hour. Then turn the oven off and leave to cool.

Before serving, bring the casserole up onto the stovetop and reheat. Add the dissolved cornflour (cornstarch) to the casserole and cook slowly until thickened. At this point, add the cut up pieces of margarine and stir into the sauce to glaze. Adjust the seasoning if necessary and serve with the Sweet Potato and Orange Purée (*see page 26*) or Exotic Pea Purée (*see page 21*).

Duck with Thyme and Bacon

This duck dish is robust, wintery and more filling with lots of beans. A good way of using up the legs nobody ate.

Serves 2

4 small or 2 large duck legs, raw or cooked
A little olive oil
1 teaspoon of fresh thyme leaves
Salt and freshly ground black pepper
1 red onion, peeled and finely sliced into rings
2 tablespoons of olive oil
6 smoked rindless bacon rashers, chopped
1 clove of garlic, peeled and crushed

455g/16oz/2½ cups of canned borlotti beans, drained
1 bay leaf
1 sprig of fresh thyme
200ml/7fl. oz/¾ cup of (GF) chicken stock
200ml/7fl. oz/¾ cup of dry white wine
A little fresh basil to decorate

Rub the raw legs with a little olive oil, 1 teaspoon of fresh thyme leaves, salt and pepper and place on half the onion. Roast for 40 minutes until crispy and cooked through.

If using cooked duck, gently cook the onion first in half the oil and when cooked through, add the legs and brush with a little more oil, salt and pepper and cook for 20 minutes until hot and crispy again.

Meanwhile, sauté the rest of the onion in a saucepan with the oil, bacon and garlic until golden. Add the borlotti beans, bay leaf and sprig of thyme, season to taste and pour over the stock and wine. Simmer for 20 minutes, stirring from time to time.

Spoon the beans and sauce onto a hot plate and place the legs on top. Sprinkle with a little shredded basil and serve with a crispy green salad.

CHAPTER 7

Buffets, Barbecues and Picnics

Chicken in Red Pesto Sauce

A couple of jars of this and that and you have a bright colourful alternative to the inevitable coronation chicken.

Serves 12

380g/13oz/1½ cups of sun dried tomato purée or paste
100g/3½oz/¾ cup of pine nuts
100g/3½oz/¾ cup of grated sheep's or goat's hard cheese (if you can eat it, omit this if not)
2 whole extra large cooked chickens
600g/21oz/2⅓ cups of (DF/GF) mayonnaise

800ml/28fl. oz/3 cups of coconut cream
Salt and freshly ground black pepper
(GF) chilli sauce/oil to taste
100ml/3fl. oz/⅓ cup of cold water
4 mild red chillies, left whole for decoration
Fresh parsley, basil or coriander (cilantro) to decorate

Put the tomato paste and pine nuts into the food processor and blend. Add the grated sheep's or goat's cheese to taste (if being used).

Strip both the chickens of their meat and discard the bones and skins. Chop into bite size pieces.

Put the meat into a big bowl and blend with the mayonnaise, red pesto sauce, and coconut cream. Season to taste with salt and pepper and chilli sauce. Add the water to loosen the mixture to a perfect consistency.

Tip the mixture into a serving dish and decorate with chillies and herbs. Serve with Wild Rice and Water Chestnut Salad or Pearl Barley Salad (*see pages 73 and 70*).

Spinach and Rice Torte

Serves 6

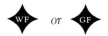 WF *or* GF

---

1 litre/1¾ pints/4 cups of (GF) vegetable stock

200g/7oz/1 cup of risotto rice and a little salt

Sea salt, freshly ground black pepper and grated nutmeg

4 tablespoons of extra virgin olive oil

125g/4oz/½ cup of (DF) margarine

2 large leeks, finely sliced

4 cloves of garlic, peeled and crushed

700g/24oz/12 cups of fresh spinach, washed and coarsely chopped

5 large free-range eggs

8 tablespoons of freshly grated pecorino (romano) cheese

4–6 tablespoons of 100% (WF) or (GF) breadcrumbs

1 teaspoon (DF) margarine

Cayenne pepper

Extra margarine to grease a 25cm/10" spring-form cake tin

Set the oven to 350°C/180°F/Gas mark 4.

Bring the stock to the boil, add the rice and cook for 20 minutes. Put into a large mixing bowl and season to taste.

Heat the oil and half the margarine in a pan. Cook the leeks until soft then stir them into the rice. Leave the fat in the pan and cook the garlic. Add the remaining margarine and gradually add in the spinach until it has wilted. Add the eggs and pecorino (romano).

Grease the tin with the extra margarine and coat in breadcrumbs. Pour the mixture into the tin. Dot the surface with the teaspoon of margarine. Sprinkle with cayenne pepper. Bake for 1 hour until golden brown and firm to touch. Cool and serve turned onto a plate at room temperature, with a crispy salad and new or baked potatoes.

Pearl Barley Salad

This is a jolly and bright salad, ideal for all age groups and all types of parties. For a bigger party, double the ingredients for 10–12, treble them for 14–18.

Serves 6

200g/7oz/1 cup of pearl barley
1 tablespoon of olive oil
500ml/16fl. oz/2 cups of (WF) vegetable stock
Pinch of saffron
The juice of 2 lemons
75ml/2½fl. oz/¼ cup of olive oil
Sea salt and freshly ground black pepper

½ cucumber, peeled, seeded and cubed
4 sun dried tomatoes, chopped
12 large black olives, stoned
2 heads of chicory, trimmed and sliced
8 spring onions (scallions), trimmed and sliced
1 red chilli, seeded and chopped
2 tablespoons of shredded basil leaves

Sauté the barley in a pan with the tablespoon of oil for a minute and then add the vegetable stock and saffron. Simmer for 45 minutes topping up with water if necessary. Drain and turn into a salad bowl.

Flavour with lemon juice, 75ml/2½fl. oz/¼ cup of oil and seasoning. Stir in the cucumber, tomatoes, olives, chicory, spring onions (scallions) and chilli. Sprinkle with basil leaves and serve with quiche and vegetable dishes.

Glazed Apricot Sausages

Venison sausages are lower in cholesterol and fat than beef and pork so I always use them for grown-up barbecues, or bangers and mash. But this works well with any type of sausage, including vegetarian.

Serves 6–12

240g/8oz ready-to-eat dried (or canned and drained) apricots
1 level teaspoon of mixed (pie) spice
1 tablespoon of (GF) Worcestershire sauce
2 teaspoons of red Thai curry paste

Salt and freshly ground black pepper
300ml/10fl. oz/1 ¼ cups of water
12–18 (GF) venison or other sausages
1 tablespoon of olive oil

Cook the apricots with the mixed (pie) spice, Worcestershire sauce, curry paste, salt and pepper in 300ml/10fl. oz/1¼ cups of water over a medium heat until soft, about 20 minutes. Add 100ml/3fl. oz/⅓ cup of water if reducing too much in the saucepan. Remove from heat and when cool process into a purée.

Place the sausages in a grill (broil)-proof tray and brush with the olive oil. Smooth over the apricot mixture and marinate for up to 24 hours.

Barbecue or grill (broil) them until cooked through and crispy on the outside.

Serve with baked potatoes.

Black Bean, Olive and Egg Salad

Preparations for this salad need to be started the day before, but it's so easy and has the bonus of being inexpensive. It is also vegetarian friendly.

Serves 12

250g/8½oz/1½ cups of black beans, soaked overnight in cold water and left covered in a cool place

1 onion studded with 2 cloves

2 bay leaves

2 sprigs of thyme

550g/19oz/4¾ cups of courgettes (zucchini), trimmed and sliced

2 large cloves of garlic, peeled and crushed

Salt and freshly ground black pepper

500g/17oz/2½ cups of sweetcorn kernels, drained (or the equivalent of frozen and defrosted sweetcorn kernels)

6 hard boiled eggs, peeled and quartered

400g/14oz/1¾ cups of black olives, stoned and halved

190g/6½oz/1½ cups of capers in vinegar, drained

200ml/7fl. oz/¾ cup of cider vinegar

300ml/10fl. oz/1¼ cups of olive oil

(GF) chilli sauce/oil to taste

1 tablespoon of caster (superfine) sugar

4 tablespoons chopped parsley

Drain the beans and cook them with the onion, bay leaves and thyme in salted boiling water until soft, probably about 1½ hours. Drain and refresh them under cold water. Transfer the beans to a huge salad bowl, remove the onion and herbs and discard.

Briefly, cook the courgettes (zucchini) in boiling water so that they are still crunchy. Refresh and drain under cold water. Add the courgettes (zucchini) garlic, salt and pepper to the beans and mix well. Leave to cool before mixing in the sweetcorn, eggs, olives and capers.

In another bowl, beat the vinegar with the oil, chilli, sugar and three quarters of the parsley. Add the dressing to the salad and mix gently. Sprinkle with the remaining parsley and serve, or chill until needed.

Wild Rice and Water Chestnut Salad

Notoriously boring rice salads always seem to be produced at parties. So I feel something a bit more original is needed to add a spark of interest to any buffet.

Serves 8

600g/21oz/3 cups of wild rice

2 mild red chillies, halved and trimmed

1 tablespoon of sesame oil

2 cloves of garlic, peeled and crushed

2 bunches of salad onions, trimmed and finely chopped

450g/16oz/2½ cups of water chestnuts, drained and roughly chopped

Salt and freshly ground black pepper

2 tablespoons of (GF) soy sauce

4 tablespoons of olive or sunflower oil

4 tablespoons of fresh coriander (cilantro) leaves

Cook the rice in boiling water until soft but not bursting. Drain and refresh under hot water. Chop up the chillies finely. Heat the sesame oil in a pan and briefly heat through the garlic and chilli. Add the onions and the chestnuts and cook for a couple of minutes. Season with salt and pepper and soy sauce before mixing in the rice. Adjust the seasoning and stir in the oil.
Mix in half the coriander (cilantro) leaves. Cover and chill. Serve with the remaining coriander (cilantro) leaves sprinkled on top.

Turkey Burgers and Black Bean Salsa

With all the beef food scares, turkey has become one of the new safe foods. The same ground rules apply: do not burn the outside, leaving the inside raw; cook slowly all the way through; don't leave the raw burgers near or in the heat, keep chilled until needed.
This is a good low fat option, and is delicious with any sort of salsa or BBQ sauce.

Serves 6–8

6 ready-made (GF) or (WF) beefburger buns or
  Corn Meal Pancakes (*see page 18*)
900g/32oz of minced fresh turkey

MARINADE
1 medium red chilli, seeded and chopped
6 trimmed spring onions (scallions), finely sliced
2 cloves of garlic, peeled and crushed
2 teaspoons of ground cumin
2 teaspoons of fresh oregano
1 teaspoon of fresh thyme
$\frac{1}{2}$ teaspoon of paprika
Salt and freshly ground black pepper
The juice of $\frac{1}{2}$ lemon

BLACK BEAN SALSA
1 small ripe fresh mango, peeled, stoned and cubed
3 spring onions (scallions), trimmed and sliced
1 clove of garlic, peeled and crushed
$\frac{1}{2}$ medium chilli, seeded and chopped
2 tablespoons of chopped coriander (cilantro)
  leaves
1 ripe tomato, skinned, seeded and chopped
The grated rind and juice of 2 limes
Salt and freshly ground black pepper
3 tablespoons of black beans (soak in water
  overnight, then boil in clean water until tender
  [about 80 minutes], drain and refresh under cold
  running water)
1 ripe avocado, peeled and chopped into the juice of
  1 lime

Mix all the marinade ingredients together in a bowl, then marinate the turkey in the marinade for a few hours.

Next make the Salsa. Place the mango, spring onions (scallions), garlic and chilli with the coriander (cilantro), tomato, lime zest and juice, salt and pepper in a food processor and mix for a second, just to bring it together.

Transfer to a clean bowl. Add the beans and the chopped avocado in juices and cover with clingfilm (plastic wrap). Chill until needed.

Now, with clean hands, divide the turkey mixture into 6 portions and shape firmly into burgers. Place on the barbecue, or char-grill in a pan until crispy and well cooked. Serve on the bun with the salsa on top or beside it.

CHAPTER 8

Desserts

Christmas Pudding

This pudding can be made up to one week in advance, which is so useful during the chaotic run-up to Christmas day.

Makes 1 very large, or 2 medium size puddings

75g/2¹/₂oz/ ¹/₃ cup of glacé cherries, chopped
175g/6oz/1 cup of candied peel, chopped
365g/12oz/2¹/₂ cups of seedless raisins
175g/6oz/1¹/₄ cups of sultanas
175g/6oz/1¹/₄ cups of currants
75g/2¹/₂oz/3¹/₄ cups of blanched almonds, chopped
250g/8¹/₂oz/4¹/₂ cups of 100% (GF) corn
    breadcrumbs or (WF) rye breadcrumbs
250g/8¹/₂oz/2 cups of (GF) shredded vegetarian suet
2 heaped teaspoons of ground cinnamon

2 heaped teaspoons of ground mixed (pie) spice
¹/₄ nutmeg, grated
¹/₂ teaspoon of ground cloves
6 large free-range eggs
The grated rind and juice of 1 orange
150ml/5fl. oz/²/₃ cup of Armagnac or brandy
3 tablespoons of rum
Sunflower oil for greasing (generously oil a 2 litre/3¹/₄
    pint/2 quarts pudding basin or 2 × 1 litre/1³/₄
    pint/1 quart basins)

Put all the dried fruit, almonds, breadcrumbs, suet and spices into a large bowl and mix together. Whisk the eggs until fluffy and thickened. Stir into the dry ingredients and then blend in the grated orange rind, juice and spirits. The mixture should just drop off the spoon. Put the mixture into the pudding basin(s). Smooth over the top and cover with a layer of double folded, oiled foil, and secure with string, making a handle to lift the basin out of the water. Stand the basin on an inverted saucer or a piece of foil folded 4 times, in a very large saucepan. Fill three quarters of the way up with water, cover with a lid or foil, and steam (6¹/₂ hours for a large pudding or 4¹/₂ hours for a smaller one). Top up with boiling water whenever necessary. When cooked, lift the basin out of the pan and allow to cool. Store in a cool dark place.

To re-heat, steam using new foil for 1¹/₂–2 hours before serving. Serve with Zabaglione (*see page 77*) or Ginger Custard (*see page 78*).

Zabaglione

An Italian favourite, Zabaglione is quick, easy and can be eaten on its own with little Coconut Crunches (see page 106) or poured over Christmas Pudding (see page 76) or Mince Pies (see page 78).

Serves 4 as a pudding or 6–8 as an accompanying sauce

4 large free-range egg yolks
70g/2½oz/⅓ cup of caster (superfine) sugar
100ml/3½fl. oz/⅓ cup of Marsala

Fill a saucepan a third of the way up with water and bring to the boil.
Put the egg yolks and sugar into a large heatproof bowl and beat together with an electric whisk. Then add the Marsala. Now put the bowl over the saucepan of simmering water and whisk on high speed until very thick. Serve immediately; either poured into warm glasses with cookies to accompany it, or with your pudding.

Mince Pies and Ginger Custard

Commercial mincemeat is often too sweet and has a less distinctive texture than home-made. This is fresh and fruity and can be made anytime, from a couple of months before Christmas to the day before.

Makes 48 pies　　　　　　　　　　　　　 *or*

MINCEMEAT

1.5kg/3.3lb of commercial vegetarian (GF/DF) mincemeat

or

175g/6oz/1¼ cups of currants
175g/6oz/1¼ cups of raisins, chopped finely
175g/6oz/1¼ cups of sultanas, chopped finely
125g/4oz/²⁄₃ cup of prunes, chopped finely
175g/6oz/1 cup of dried apples, chopped finely
125g/4oz/²⁄₃ cup of glacé cherries, chopped finely
125g/4oz/¹⁄₃ cup of candied peel, chopped finely
250g/8½oz/2 cups of (GF) vegetarian suet
300g/10½oz/1½ cups of light brown muscovado sugar
1 teaspoon of ground cloves
2 teaspoons of mixed (pie) spice
The freshly grated rind and juice of 2 lemons
250ml/8fl. oz/1 cup of Grand Marnier
1 ripe pear, peeled, cored and chopped
125g/4oz of fresh cranberries, chopped

PASTRY

330g/11oz/2¹⁄₃ cups of (WF) rye flour or (GF) millet flour
330g/11oz/2¹⁄₃ cups of rice flour
330g/11oz/2 cups of finely processed (WF) oats or (GF) maize flour
500g/17oz/2¼ cups of (DF) margarine
½ teaspoon of salt
2 large free-range egg yolks, mixed with a little cold water
6–8 tablespoons of water

FINISHING TOUCHES

(DF) margarine and (GF) flour for tin
Icing (confectioner's) sugar, caster (superfine) sugar and ground cinnamon for dusting

GINGER CUSTARD

For 6–8 people (double the quantities for 12–16 people)
6 large free-range egg yolks
100g/3½oz/½ cup of caster (superfine) sugar
1 level tablespoon of (GF) cornflour (cornstarch)
3 tablespoons of stem ginger syrup
600ml/20fl. oz/2½ cups of unsweetened soya milk
3 tablespoons of ginger wine, or rum

Set the oven to 180°/350°F/Gas mark 4.

To make the mincemeat, put all of the dried fruit, cherries and candied peel into a large mixing bowl. Add the suet, sugar, spices, lemon rind and juice, and then the Grand Marnier. Leave in a cold place for 2 days, ensuring it is always covered.
Stir the mincemeat thoroughly and add more liqueur if not moist. Spoon the mixture into sterilized jars, cover and store or use now to make the mince pies by adding the finishing touches

(mix in the chopped pear and chopped cranberries before filling the pies).

To make the pastry mix all of the ingredients (except the water) in the food processor and blend for a few seconds until it starts to gather together to form a dough, and then add the water. Put the mixture onto a floured board and knead lightly into a firm dough.

Wrap in clingfilm (plastic wrap) and chill for 30 minutes. Roll out onto a floured board a quarter of the dough at a time and cut with a pastry cutter into 48 7cm/2³/₄" circles (for the bases) and 48 5cm/2" circles (for the lids).

Add little drops of extra water if it is too dry and crumbly.

Grease and flour 48 non-stick patty tins and line with the pastry circles. Fill with a large teaspoon of mincemeat and cover with the lids. Sprinkle with caster (superfine) sugar and cinnamon and bake for 25 minutes until golden. Leave to cool slightly before easing out of the tins and onto a wire rack. Store in an airtight container until needed. Warm through before serving and dust with sifted icing (confectioner's) sugar.

To make the custard, mix the egg yolks, sugar, cornflour (cornstarch) and ginger syrup in a large mixing bowl.

Warm the milk in a non-stick saucepan and then gradually stir into the bowl of eggs. Transfer the mixture back to the saucepan and cook very gently over a low heat, stirring most of the time, until you have a thick and smooth custard. Add the ginger wine. Remove from the heat just as it reaches boiling point – do not boil. Pour into a clean bowl and stir from time to time, as it cools slightly. Serve in 2 warm sauceboats with the mince pies or Christmas pudding.

Lime Meringue Pie

A nice change from lemon, which has become so commercialized. Serve with coconut cream as an alternative to cream, or with a (DF) vanilla ice cream.

Serves 6

125g/4oz/¹/₂ cup of (DF) margarine
100g/3¹/₂oz/³/₄ cup of rice flour
75g/2¹/₂oz/¹/₂ cup of maize flour
25g/³/₄oz of caster (superfine) sugar
1 large free-range egg yolk beaten with 2 teaspoons
   of cold water
The grated rind, pulp and juice 5 limes
The juice of 2 lemons
75g/2¹/₂oz/¹/₂ cup of caster (superfine) sugar
4 level tablespoons of (GF) cornflour (cornstarch)

3 large free-range egg yolks
25g/³/₄oz of (DF) margarine

MERINGUE
3 egg whites
175g/6oz of caster (superfine) sugar

Ceramic baking balls and greaseproof (wax) paper

Preheat the oven to 190°C/375°F/Gas mark 5.

Make the pastry by mixing the 125g/4oz/¹/₂ cup of margarine with both the flours and 25g/³/₄oz of caster sugar in a food processor for a few seconds. Add the egg yolk and water mixture until you have a firm dough. Knead briefly on a floured board and roll out enough pastry to line a 24cm/9¹/₂" fluted non-stick flan tin.
Bake blind with a layer of greaseproof (wax) paper and ceramic balls, until golden (about 25 minutes). Remove the paper and balls.
Meanwhile make the filling. Put the lime rind, pulp and juice and the lemon juice into a saucepan with 60ml/2fl. oz/¹/₄ cup of water and 75g/2¹/₂oz/¹/₂ cup of sugar and heat gently until the sugar has dissolved.
Mix the cornflour (cornstarch) into a smooth paste with 5 tablespoons of cold water and then stir the mixture into the juices quickly. Now increase the heat and bring to the boil, stirring all the time. Cook for 1–2 minutes only. Cool and then beat in the 3 egg yolks and 25g/³/₄oz of the margarine. Pour it into the prepared pastry.
Turn the oven heat down to 150°C/300°F/Gas mark 2.
Now make the meringue by whisking the egg whites until stiff. Then whisk in half the sugar and fold in the remaining sugar with a metal spoon. Pile on top of the lime pie and bake for 35 minutes until golden. Serve warm.

Treacle Tart

Corn flakes are an easy breadcrumb substitute and work very well in this traditional pudding. Outrageous with Praline Ice Cream (see page 97)!

Serves 6

110g/3³/₄oz/³/₄ cup of rice flour
100g/3¹/₂oz/³/₄ cup of maize flour
¹/₄ teaspoon of salt
150g/5oz/²/₃ cup of (DF) margarine
1 large egg yolk

3 heaped tablespoons of crushed corn flakes
The grated rind of 1 lemon
The juice of ¹/₂ lemon
7 rounded tablespoons of golden (corn) syrup

Set the oven at 180°C/350°F/Gas mark 4.

Grease and flour a fluted tart tin (23cm/9").
Sift the flours and salt into a mixing bowl. Cut the margarine into this using a blunt knife. Mix in the egg yolk and a little cold water.
Bring to a ball with floured fingers and then knead briefly on a floured board and roll out thickly.
Gently lift the pastry over the tart tin and press with your fingers to fit neatly. Trim the edges.
Sprinkle the corn flakes over the base and spoon over the lemon rind and juice.
Evenly distribute the syrup over it and bake in the oven for 25 minutes.
Let it get cold before serving warmed-up, otherwise it will be too crumbly. You can add chopped stem ginger for a change in the winter or serve with Stem Ginger Ice Cream (*see page 91*).

Hot Chocolate Soufflé

If, like me, you always have chocolate and eggs in the fridge, this is a wonderful emergency pudding worth its weight in gold when impromptu guests arrive!

Serves 4–6

30g/1oz of (DF) margarine
30g/1oz of rice flour
200ml/7fl. oz/³/₄ cup of soya milk
2 tablespoons of Cointreau or any orange liqueur
1 tablespoon of caster (superfine) sugar

150g/5oz of (DF/GF) luxury dark chocolate, broken up
4 large free-range egg yolks
6 egg whites
Pinch of salt

Preheat the oven to 200°C/400°F/Gas mark 6.

Grease a 1½ litre/2 pint/3 US pint soufflé dish with extra (DF) margarine and dust with a little extra caster sugar.

Melt the margarine in a saucepan. Sift in the flour and gradually beat in the milk. Bring to the boil, stirring all the time. When the sauce is thick and smooth, add the Cointreau, a tablespoon of caster (superfine) sugar and the chocolate pieces. Remove from the heat and stir until the chocolate has melted and blended with the other ingredients. Mix in the egg yolks.

Now whisk the egg whites, with a pinch of salt, in a bowl until stiff. Stir 1 spoonful of the egg whites into the chocolate mixture and then fold in the rest with a metal spoon.

Turn the mixture into the soufflé dish and bake for 30 minutes until puffed, but just firm in the centre. Serve immediately.

Apple and Blackberry Crumble

A good old-fashioned pudding: delicious served with Coconut Ice Cream (see page 96) or Ginger Custard (see page 78).

Serves 6

4 large cooking apples

4 tablespoons of sugar

1 teaspoon of mixed (pie) spice

The juice of ½ a lemon

500g/16½oz/3½ cups of fresh or frozen blackberries

1 teaspoon of (DF) margarine

CRUMBLE

120g/4oz/½ cup of (DF) margarine

60g/2oz/⅓ cup of sugar

60g/2oz/⅓ cup of oats

100g/3½oz/¾ cup of rice flour

60g/2oz/½ cup of millet flakes

1 teaspoon of ground cinnamon

Set the oven at 180°C/350°F/Gas mark 4.

Peel and core the apples and slice finely into a saucepan with the sugar, mixed (pie) spice and lemon juice. Cook gently until soft. Add the blackberries and remove from the heat. Dot with margarine.

Next make the crumble using the food processor by mixing the margarine with the sugar for a few seconds. Add the oats, rice, flour, millet flakes and cinnamon and whiz briefly together.

Put the apple mixture into a deep 30cm/12" ovenproof dish, cover with crumble and bake in the centre of the oven for 25 minutes, or until golden and bubbling.

Coconut Rice Moulds with Passion Fruit Sauce

This is an exotic pudding, ideal after an Asian or Indian main course. You can substitute this sauce for mango, apricot or any seasonal soft berries that purée well.

Serves 6

125g/4oz/²/₃ cup of pudding rice	SAUCE
400ml/14fl. oz/1½ cups of water	The juice of 1 lemon
400ml/14fl. oz/1½ cups of coconut milk	4 passion fruit, halved and scooped out
20g/³/₄oz of caster (superfine) sugar	1 large ripe mango, peeled, sliced and puréed
11g/½oz of gelatine	
200ml/7fl. oz/³/₄ cup of coconut cream	Ramekins and clingfilm (plasticwrap)
2 egg whites with a pinch of salt	
Fresh mint leaves to decorate	

Put the rice and water into a large saucepan and bring to the boil. Then cook gently for 10 minutes.

Add the coconut milk and sugar and simmer for another 35 minutes until it is soft, thick and creamy. Stir from time to time to prevent the rice sticking to the pan.

Prepare the gelatine by dissolving it in 100ml/3fl. oz/⅓ cup of boiling water and mixing until it is clear. Stir the gelatine into the rice and fold in the coconut cream. Beat the egg whites and gently fold in with a metal spoon.

Now line 6 ramekins with clingfilm (plastic wrap). Then spoon the rice pudding into them and smooth over the surfaces. Chill for about 4 hours until set.

Make the passion fruit sauce by mixing the lemon juice and passion fruit pulp with the mango purée and a little extra water until it is the right consistency. Chill until needed.

To serve, turn the rice puddings out on to 6 plates and remove the clingfilm (plastic wrap). Pour some of the sauce over and around them and decorate with a sprig of fresh mint.

Hot Pear Brownie

Chocolate and pears are always a good combination, hot or cold. This is a slightly healthier version of other sticky puddings.

Serves 6

820g/30oz/4 cups of pears in fruit juice
75g/2¹/₂oz/¹/₂ cup of rice flour
A pinch of salt
1 teaspoon of (GF) baking powder
75g/2¹/₂oz/¹/₃ cup of (DF) margarine
¹/₂ teaspoon of vanilla essence

75g/2¹/₂oz/¹/₃ cup of dark (DF) chocolate
175g/6oz/³/₄ cup of caster (superfine) sugar
2 large free-range eggs, beaten
75g/2¹/₂oz/²/₃ cup of chopped pecans

Set the oven at 180°C/350°F/Gas mark 4.

Grease a deep baking dish. Cover the base with the pears.
Sift the flour, salt and baking powder into a bowl. Put the margarine, vanilla essence and chocolate into a saucepan, stir until melted and then remove from the heat.
Beat in the sugar, eggs and pecans. Stir the chocolate mixture into the dry ingredients, pour the batter over the pears and bake in the centre of the oven for about 35 minutes or until the brownie mix is just firm.
Serve warm with (DF) ice cream or Zabaglione (*see page 77*) for a dinner party.

Pear Tart Tatin

French chefs use pears or apples for this lovely pudding. It is heavenly served with home-made (DF) vanilla ice cream.

Serves 6

PASTRY

100g/3¹/₂oz/³/₄ cup of rice flour
75g/2¹/₂oz/¹/₂ cup of maize flour
55g/2oz/¹/₃ cup of ground rice
140g/5oz/¹/₃ cup of (DF) margarine
55g/2oz/¹/₃ cup of caster (superfine)sugar
1 large free-range egg, beaten

TOPPING

100g/3¹/₂oz/¹/₂ cup of (DF) margarine
140g/5oz/³/₄ cup of granulated sugar
1050g/37oz/7¹/₂ cups of ripe pears, peeled, cored and quartered
The grated rind of 1 lemon

Tart Tatin dish, or a 25cm/10" wide and 6cm/2¹/₂" deep round tin

Preheat the oven to 200°C/400°F/Gas mark 6.

To make the pastry sift the flours and ground rice together into a large bowl. Then rub in the margarine until it resembles fine breadcrumbs. Stir in the sugar and add the egg. Mix until you have binding dough. Wrap in clingfilm (plastic wrap) and chill until needed.
Next make the topping. Gently melt the margarine in a large frying pan with the sugar.
Turn up the heat to high and once the margarine and sugar have started to boil add the pears to the pan. Sprinkle the lemon rind over the pears.
Cook until the margarine starts to caramelize. Remove from the heat.
Put all the pears with the caramel into the dish. Roll out the pastry on a floured board into a thick circle, to fit the top of the pan. Lay it on top of the pears and press down slightly.
Bake in the oven for 10 minutes and then reduce the oven temperature to 190°C/375°C/Gas mark 5 and bake for a further 10 minutes, until golden and bubbling.
Allow to cool slightly before turning onto a warm plate and serving.

Summer Fruit Mousse

This is a light and colourful pudding that can be made with frozen fruit throughout the year.

Serves 8

500g/16¹/₂oz/2 cups of mixed summer fruits (frozen or fresh)

100g/3¹/₂oz/¹/₂ cup of caster (superfine) sugar

The grated rind and juice of 1 lemon

2 tablespoons of gelatine, soaked in 3 tablespoons of boiling water until dissolved and clear

200ml/7fl. oz/³/₄ cup of coconut cream

200ml/7fl. oz/³/₄ cup of soya cream

2 egg whites

FOR DECORATION

1 egg white

125g/4oz/¹/₂ cup of fresh summer berries

Caster (superfine) sugar

Put the fruit in a saucepan with the sugar, lemon rind and juice. Cook for 5 minutes or until just soft. Add the gelatine and remove from the heat. Sieve into a bowl and leave to cool.

When cool, place in the fridge until it begins to set. Fold in the coconut cream and soya cream. Whisk the egg whites until stiff and then fold into the mousse with a metal spoon. Spoon this into a pretty glass bowl and smooth over. Chill until set.

Decorate at the last minute. Lightly whisk the egg white. Discard half of it. Dip the fresh fruit in the remaining egg white and then coat with sugar. Arrange on top of the mousse and serve.

Chocolate Sachetorte

This is a dreamy Viennese cake, which is eaten in cafés all over the city with steaming cups of coffee or hot chocolate.

Serves 8

300g/11oz/2 cups of dark (DF) chocolate and a little extra chocolate for decoration

175g/6oz/³/₄ cup of (DF) margarine

125g/4oz/¹/₂ cup of caster (superfine) sugar

100g/3¹/₂oz/1¹/₃ cups of ground almonds

4 large free-range eggs, separated

50g/2oz/1 cup of 100% pure (WF) rye or (GF) corn breadcrumbs

2 tablespoon of sugar-free apricot or raspberry jam (jelly)

50g/2oz/¹/₃ cup of icing (confectioner's) sugar

2 tablespoons of black coffee

Set the oven to 180°C/350°F/Gas mark 4.

Grease a 23cm/9" spring release cake tin with some extra margarine and line with greaseproof (wax) paper.

Break half the chocolate into a bowl and microwave until just melting and then stir until smooth.

Cream 125g/4oz/¹/₂ cup of the margarine and the sugar together in a bowl. Stir in the almonds, egg yolks and breadcrumbs, then fold in the melted chocolate and beat well.

Whisk the egg whites until stiff and then fold half at a time into the chocolate mixture. Pour into the prepared cake tin. Bake the cake for 40 minutes until firm to the touch. Allow to cool for 45 minutes and then turn out onto a serving plate. Brush the cake with the jam (jelly).

Melt the remaining chocolate and margarine together in a bowl in the microwave. Stir and sift in the icing (confectioner's) sugar and then beat in the black coffee. Leave to stand for 5 minutes. Spread the icing all over the cake. Coarsely grate some extra chocolate on top of the cake and serve chilled.

Amaretto Tipsy Trifle

A boozy trifle for any time of year. Ideal after a roast for Sunday lunch or at Christmas. You can substitute raspberries with any fruit such as apricots, bananas or blackberries.

Serves 6

100g/3½oz/⅔ cup of rice flour

75g/2½oz/½ cup of maize flour

3 level teaspoons of (GF) baking powder

100g/3½oz/½ cup of (DF) margarine

100g/3½oz/1¼ cups of ground almonds

2 large free-range eggs

4 tablespoons of apple juice

1 teaspoon of vanilla essence

50ml/2fl. oz/¼ cup of Amaretto di Saronno liqueur

CUSTARD

3 large free-range egg yolks

1 heaped teaspoon of (GF) cornflour (cornstarch)

1 teaspoon of pure vanilla essence

2 tablespoons of Amaretto di Saronno liqueur

250ml/8fl. oz/1 cup of soya cream

200ml/7fl. oz/¾ cup of coconut cream

Some extra Amaretto liqueur

340g/12oz/1 cup of sugar-free raspberry jam (jelly)

2 large bananas, peeled, trimmed and sliced

250g/9oz/2¼ cups of fresh or frozen (defrosted) raspberries

70g/2½oz/⅔ cup of (GF/DF) Amaretto di Saronno biscuits (cookies), crumbled

String

Grease a 1 litre/1¾ pint/1 quart pudding basin with extra margarine and grease some greaseproof (wax) paper. Have string ready.

Sift the flours and baking powder together in a bowl. In a food processor, mix the margarine, almonds, eggs, juice, vanilla essence and Amaretto until smooth. Quickly blend the flours into this mixture. Scrape into the pudding basin. Cover with the greaseproof (wax) paper and secure with string around the top, making a handle to remove the basin from the pan later.

Half-fill a saucepan with boiling water and simmer the pudding for 1 hour until firm. Lift the basin out of the pan and leave to cool. Turn out the sponge and cut it into thin slices.

Now make the custard. Mix the egg yolks, cornflour (cornstarch), vanilla essence and Amaretto together with the soya cream and coconut cream. Cook very gently in a non-stick pan, stirring all the time, until it comes to the boil. Immediately remove the pan from the heat and allow to cool, stirring occasionally.

Use a pretty glass bowl and arrange a layer of sponge slices around the base and sides, sprinkle with extra Amaretto di Saronno liqueur. Spread all over with three quarters of the jam (jelly) and then put the bananas on the bottom. Pour over half of the custard. Cover with the remaining sponge and spread the rest of the jam (jelly) over the sponge and top with all the raspberries. Cover with the remaining custard, sprinkle with the crumbled Amaretto di Saronno biscuits (cookies), and chill until needed.

Double Chocolate Chip Ice Cream

Totally sinful ice cream! For extra calories serve with cookies or Chocolate Brownies (see page 101).

Serves 4

4 large free-range egg yolks
1 heaped teaspoon of (GF) cornflour (cornstarch)
1 heaped tablespoon of sugar
300ml/10fl. oz/1¼ cups of soya milk

3 tablespoons of (GF) cocoa powder, sieved
250ml/8fl. oz/1 cup of soya cream
100g/3½oz/⅔ cup of (DF) dark chocolate chips or chopped pieces

Mix the egg yolks, cornflour (cornstarch) and sugar together in a bowl. Gradually add the milk. Now transfer this mixture into a non-stick saucepan and cook over a low heat, stirring most of the time until thick – but do not boil.

Remove the pan from the heat and stir in the cocoa powder and soya cream. Sieve the custard into a bowl and leave to cool.

When it is cold and the ice cream maker is ready, mix in the chocolate chips or pieces and churn in the machine until frozen, but still soft enough to scrape out of the mixer. Freeze in a sealable container until needed, or serve immediately with cookies.

THE SENSITIVE GOURMET

Stem Ginger Ice Cream

For a glamorous pudding make Brandy Snap Baskets (see page 103), or Stem Ginger Cookies (see page 105), serve with this ice cream and decorate with fresh fruit and mint leaves.

Serves 4

1 teaspoon of ground ginger	300ml/10fl. oz/1¼ cups of soya milk
4 large free-range egg yolks	6 stem ginger, finely chopped
1 heaped teaspoon of (GF) cornflour (cornstarch)	3 tablespoons of stem ginger syrup
1 heaped tablespoon of sugar	250ml/8fl. oz/1 cup of soya cream

Mix the ground ginger, egg yolks, cornflour (cornstarch) and sugar together in a bowl and gradually incorporate the milk. Transfer to a non-stick saucepan and, stirring all the time, cook over a low heat until thick and creamy – but do not boil.

Remove from the heat and add the ginger, syrup and lastly the soya cream.

Following the instructions on your ice cream maker, churn until the custard is frozen and serve.

Raspberry Gallette

Making pastry on a marble board keeps everything lovely and cool and gives excellent results. If you are in a hurry, you can fill the gallette with suitable (DF) vanilla ice cream and raspberries and serve before it melts!

Serves 8

225g/8oz/1⅔ cups of rice flour, sifted
35g/1¼oz/⅓ cup of ground almonds
50g/1¾oz/⅓ cup of icing (confectioner's) sugar
120g/4oz/½ cup of (DF) margarine
The grated rind of 1 orange
2 large free-range egg yolks
1 teaspoon of orange flower water

15g/½oz of (DF) margarine
Enough coconut cream to make the crème
  spreadable

500g/16½oz/4 cups of fresh raspberries
Icing (confectioner's) sugar to dust
Mint leaves and spare raspberries to decorate

CRÈME PATISSIERE
3 large free-range egg yolks
40g/1¼oz/⅕ cup of caster (superfine) sugar
½ teaspoon of almond essence
1 tablespoon of (GF) cornflour (cornstarch)
250ml/8fl. oz/1 cup of soya milk

COULIS
500g/16½oz/4 cups of mixed red summer fruit
The juice of ½ lemon
Rum and water
Icing (confectioner's) sugar, to sweeten (optional)

Set the oven at 180°C/350°F/Gas mark 4.

Place the flour, almonds, sugar, margarine and orange rind into a food processor and blend until it resembles fine breadcrumbs. Briefly, mix in the egg yolks and orange flower water.
Wrap the dough in clingfilm (plastic wrap) and chill for 1 hour. Divide the pastry in half and roll it out thinly. Use a 23cm/9" plate as a template to cut out 2 circles and place on a baking sheet. Mark each circle into 8 wedges, scored almost through the pastry. Bake for 20 minutes until golden. Transfer to a wire rack to cool.
Make the crème patissiere. Put the egg yolks, sugar, essence and flour in a bowl and mix. Gradually beat in the milk and then transfer the mixture to a non-stick saucepan. Gently cook over a low heat, bringing it slowly to the boil. Keep stirring all the time until it is smooth and thick. Transfer to a bowl and dot with margarine to stop a skin forming. When cold, mix in the coconut cream until spreadable. Spread the cream all over the pastry circles and set on a plate. Cover with raspberries and then the top layer of pastry. Dust with icing (confectioner's) sugar and decorate the plate with a few mint leaves and raspberries.
Make the coulis. Purée the fruit with the lemon juice and enough rum/water to make into spooning consistency – sweeten to taste if necessary with icing (confectioner's) sugar. Serve the coulis with the gallette.

THE SENSITIVE GOURMET

Strawberry Shortcake

English strawberries are so wonderful in the summer and this is such an English-style pudding!

Serves 6

30g/1oz of sugar

130g/4¹/₂oz/1 cup of rice flour

100g/3¹/₂oz/³/₄ cup of millet flour

1 tablespoon of (GF) baking powder

¹/₄ teaspoon of salt

60g/2oz/¹/₄ cup of (DF) margarine

3 teaspoons of rosewater

5 tablespoons of plain goat's yoghurt or soya
  yoghurt, beaten with 3 large eggs

4 tablespoons of redcurrent jelly, warmed in a
  saucepan

750ml/25fl. oz/3¹/₄ cups of (DF) vanilla ice cream

500g/17oz/3¹/₂ cups of strawberries, rinsed
  thoroughly and sliced

Grease and flour a 23cm/9" diameter cake tin, and
  line with baking parchment (wax paper).

Set the oven at 200°/400°F/Gas mark 6.

Sift the dry ingredients together in a bowl and rub (cut) in the margarine until it resembles breadcrumbs. Lightly mix the rosewater, yoghurt and eggs together and blend into the dry ingredients.

Scrape the mixture into the prepared cake tin and bake for about 20 minutes, or until golden brown. Cool and then split open the shortcake with a long knife.

Gently heat the redcurrent jelly in a saucepan until melted and then keep warm.

Put the shortcake base on a plate and brush with half of the warm redcurrant jelly. When the shortcake is cold, spoon on softened vanilla ice cream and cover with half of the strawberries. Place the remaining cake on top, add the rest of the strawberries and brush with the warm jelly to glaze. Serve immediately.

Chestnut and Chocolate Roulade

This is a quick and easy Christmas pudding to make. You can transform it into a Yule log by covering it with chocolate icing, dusting it with icing (confectioner's) sugar and adding a festive spring of holly.

Serves 6

5 large free-range eggs, separated
175g/6oz/1 cup of caster (superfine) sugar
150g/5oz/1 cup of (DF) dark chocolate
3 tablespoons of cold water
½ teaspoon of pure vanilla essence
225g/8oz/1 cup of unsweetened chestnut purée
240g/8½oz/1¼ cups of whole chestnuts, drained and
    roughly chopped

2 tablespoons of brandy, or rum, or fresh black
    coffee
2 tablespoons of coconut cream
(GF) cocoa powder (or grated [DF] dark
    chocolate), to dust

Grease and line a large roulade tin with greaseproof
    (wax) paper

Preheat the oven to 180°C/350°F/Gas mark 4.

Beat the egg yolks in a bowl with the sugar until pale and fluffy. Melt the chocolate in a bowl set over boiling water in the microwave. Stir the chocolate into the egg yolks. Add the cold water and vanilla essence.
Whisk the egg whites until soft peaks are formed and then fold into the chocolate mixture.
Spread over the tray, leaving a 2.5cm/1" border all round.
Bake until firm and spongy, about 15 minutes.
Set the roulade tin on a wire rack and cover with a clean damp cloth until cold.
Remove the cloth and loosen the paper. Dust another sheet of greaseproof (wax) paper with cocoa and turn the roulade onto it. Peel off the paper. Blend together the chestnut purée, brandy, rum or coffee and coconut cream until smooth and spreadable. Mix in the chopped chestnuts and spread all over the roulade.
Roll-up the roulade using the paper beneath it to guide you and serve decorated with extra cocoa or grated chocolate.

Plum Frangipani Tart

You can make this recipe with apricots in season, or even with greengages.

Serves 6

PASTRY
1 heaped tablespoon of icing (confectioner's) sugar
Pinch of salt
75g/2½oz/½ cup of rice flour
75g/2½oz/½ cup of millet flour
75g/2½oz/½ cup of maize flour
150g/5oz/⅔ cup of (DF) margarine
1 large free-range egg yolk

FRANGIPANE CREAM
75g/2½oz/⅓ cup of caster (superfine) sugar
75g/2½oz/⅓ cup of (DF) margarine
50g/1¾oz/⅓ cup of rice flour

2 large free-range eggs
150g/5oz/1¾ cups of ground almonds
1 tablespoon of orange flower water
½ teaspoon of almond essence

TOPPING
900g/32oz of fresh ripe plums, halved and stones
   (pits) removed

GLAZE
3 tablespoons of runny plum or apricot jam (jelly)
2 tablespoons of Amaretto di Saronno liqueur

Set the oven at 190°C/375°F/Gas mark 5.

First make the pastry. Mix all the ingredients briefly in a food processor until it comes together into a ball. Scrape out. Wrap up in clingfilm (plastic wrap) and chill for 30 minutes. Then roll out the pastry to fit a 25.5cm/10" lightly greased and floured loose-bottomed fluted flan tin. Cover with greaseproof (wax) paper and ceramic beans and bake blind for 20 minutes. Remove the beans and paper.

For the frangipane cream, mix all the ingredients briefly in a food processor until they are thick but not stiff. Add more orange water if necessary.

Cook the plums with a little water in a covered pan over a medium heat until a little softer and carefully drain off the juices.

Fill the cooked pastry shell with the frangipane cream and smooth over the top. Lay the plums, cut side down over the cream, starting around the edge and working into the middle. Bake for 40 minutes or until golden. Warm the jam (jelly) and Amaretto together and brush all over the tart. Serve warm.

Coconut Ice Cream

To make this a tropical concoction serve with an exotic fruit purée, such as mango, lime juice and passion fruit liquidized together with a little rum, instead of the chocolate sauce.

Serves 6

CHOCOLATE SAUCE
150g/5oz/1 cup of (DF) dark chocolate
100ml/3fl. oz/⅓ cup of weak black coffee
150ml/5fl. oz/⅔ cup of warm water
2 tablespoons of Amaretto di Saronno liqueur
3 heaped tablespoons of (GF) cocoa
2 heaped teaspoons of caster (superfine) sugar

ICE CREAM
4 large free-range egg yolks
1 heaped teaspoon of (GF) cornflour (cornstarch)
2 heaped tablespoons of caster (superfine) sugar
400ml/14fl. oz/1½ cups of coconut milk
5 heaped tablespoons of desiccated coconut
200ml/7fl. oz/¾ cup of coconut cream
2 tablespoons of toasted coconut pieces (from health food shops)

Make the chocolate sauce by slowly melting together all the ingredients in a non-stick saucepan. Stir until thick and creamy. Remove from the heat and cover until needed.

Make the ice cream by mixing the egg yolks, cornflour (cornstarch) and sugar together in a bowl, and slowly adding the coconut milk. Transfer to a saucepan, add the desiccated coconut and cook over a low heat, stirring all the time. Cook until thick and smooth then remove from the heat and transfer to a bowl. Stir in the coconut cream.

Once it is cool, pour the custard into your prepared ice cream maker and churn until frozen and smooth (probably about 20 minutes).

Serve scoops of ice cream scattered with toasted coconut pieces with a pool of lukewarm chocolate sauce beside it.

Praline Ice Cream

This is the ice cream I miss most as I always see it in the supermarkets. It is ideal with any fruit or for dinner parties scooped into meringue baskets or Brandy Snaps (see page 103).

Serves 6

50g/2oz/¼ cup of caster (superfine) sugar
50g/2oz/½ cup of chopped blanched almonds
1 level teaspoon (GF) cornflour (cornstarch)
4 large free-range egg yolks

300ml/10fl. oz/1¼ cups of soya milk
1 vanilla pod, split
250ml/8fl. oz/1 cup of soya cream
1 teaspoon of pure vanilla essence

Make the praline first by quickly melting the sugar with the almonds in a saucepan until they turn dark golden brown. Leave this mixture to cool. When the praline is cold put it into a plastic bag and bash with a rolling pin until it resembles breadcrumbs (alternatively grind to a powder in a food processor).

Now make the ice cream by quickly mixing the cornflour (cornstarch) with the egg yolks and a little of the milk until you have a smooth paste. Continue adding the milk and then pour the liquid into a saucepan to cook. Add the vanilla pod and then stir continuously until the custard is very thick and hot – but do not boil.

Remove the pan from the heat and take out the pod (wash it under warm water and dry on absorbent paper so that you can re-use it).

Now add the cream and blend briefly. Mix in the vanilla essence and the praline and leave to cool.

Follow the instructions on your ice cream maker and pour in the custard. Churn until frozen and then serve, or freeze in a sealable container.

CHAPTER 9

Teatime Baking

Sesame Flapjacks

Flapjacks are ideal for picnics because they don't break up easily and they are filling, chewy and healthy. I've included instructions for drizzling with dark chocolate for a naughty snack!

Makes 24

200g/7oz/1 cup of (DF) margarine
300g/10½oz/1 cup of golden (corn) syrup
450g/15½oz/5⅓ cups of porridge oats
Pinch of salt
1 heaped tablespoon of sesame seeds

1 tablespoon of finely chopped stem ginger
 (optional) or 1 heaped teaspoon of ground
 cinnamon with 100g/3½oz/¾ cup of mincemeat
 (optional – ideal for Christmas)
150g/5oz/1 cup of dark (DF) chocolate

Set the oven at 180°C/350°F/Gas mark 4.

Melt the margarine with the syrup in a saucepan over a low heat, or in the microwave.
Add the oats, salt and sesame seeds, and the stem ginger or the cinnamon and mincemeat if using.
Turn into an oiled baking tin and press down with the back of a spoon.
Bake in the centre of the oven for about 25 minutes, or until golden brown.
Gently heat the chocolate and 2 tablespoons of water together in a bowl over a pan of boiling water. When it is the right consistency, drizzle the mixture over the flapjacks.
Cut into squares whilst hot, but allow to cool completely before removing from the tin to store or serve.

Chocolate Brownies

My absolute favourite! Chewy brownies with (DF) vanilla ice cream was my daily fix when I lived in New York.

Serves 6

75g/2¹/₂oz/¹/₃ cup of (DF) margarine

100g/3¹/₂oz/²/₃ cup of (DF) dark chocolate

175g/6oz/1 cup of caster (superfine) sugar

2 large free-range eggs, beaten

75g/2¹/₂oz/¹/₂ cup of rice flour

1 level teaspoon of (GF) baking powder

¹/₄ teaspoon of salt

¹/₂ teaspoon of vanilla essence

75g/2¹/₂oz/²/₃ cup of pecan nuts, chopped

Grease a 28cm/11" rectangular non-stick baking tin with a little sunflower oil

Preheat the oven to 180°C/350°F/Gas mark 4.

Melt the margarine and chocolate in a saucepan over a very low heat, stirring constantly. Remove from the heat, add the sugar and allow to cool slightly.

Mix in the beaten eggs, then sift in the flour, baking powder and salt and fold in the vanilla essence and the chopped nuts.

Pour the mixture into the baking tin and bake for 30 minutes. Test with an inserted skewer that it is just cooked through (the skewer should come out clean).

Cool in the tin and cut into squares.

Chocolate Chip and Brazil Nut Cookies

Brilliant bribery for children of all ages! You can vary the chocolate chips if you can eat milk and white chocolate and you can vary the nuts to peanuts, hazelnuts, pecans or walnuts. For a nut free version, use chopped dried apricots or other fruit or berries with seeds.

Makes 24

75g/2½oz/½ cup of white rice flour
50g/1¾oz/⅓ cup of maize flour
½ teaspoon of bicarbonate of soda (baking soda)
50g/1¾oz/¼ cup of soft brown sugar
50g/1¾oz/¼ cup of vanilla sugar (or add ½ teaspoon of vanilla essence to ordinary sugar)

75g/2½oz/⅓ cup of (DF) margarine
1 large free-range egg
60g/2oz/⅓ cup of chopped Brazil nuts
100g/3½oz/⅔ cup of (DF) dark chocolate, chopped into small pieces

Set the oven at 180°C/350°F/Gas mark 4.

Combine the first 7 ingredients in a food processor and blend for a few seconds. Mix in the nuts and chocolate.

Spoon small mounds of the mixture onto greased baking sheets and keep them well spaced out. Bake the cookies for 10–12 minutes until golden brown. Lift them off and place them on a wire rack to cool.

Brandy Snaps

I serve these brandy snaps with my own ice cream. The baskets are brilliant for summer dinner parties filled with a scoop of Stem Ginger Ice Cream (see page 91), with fresh rasberries and a sprig of fresh mint to decorate.

Serves 6–7 (2 brandy snaps each, or about 8 baskets)

Oil for greasing
50g/1½oz/¼ cup of (DF) margarine
50g/1½oz/¼ cup of caster (superfine) sugar
2 tablespoons of golden (corn) syrup

50g/1½oz/⅓ cup of white rice flour
1 level teaspoon of ground ginger
1 teaspoon of brandy or lemon juice
The grated rind of ½ lemon

Preheat the oven to 180°C/350°F/Gas mark 4.

Grease the handles of several wooden spoons or the outsides of 6 upturned ramekins. Line 2 or 3 baking sheets with baking parchment (wax paper).

Melt the margarine with the sugar and the syrup in a small saucepan over a low heat. Remove from the heat and stir in the flour and ginger, brandy or lemon juice and lemon rind.

Place small spoonfuls about 5cm/2" apart on the baking sheets to allow for spreading during baking. Cook until golden and bubbly.

Cool for ½ minute and then speedily loosen them with a greased palette knife and wrap around either the spoon handles or the ramekin bases.

Leave to set and then carefully slide them off. If they are too brittle then briefly re-warm in the oven and try again.

They are now ready to serve or store in an airtight container.

Sesame Corn Crackers

These savoury biscuits are very handy for dips, and to accompany soups or salads. They are also ideal for nibbling along with drinks or cocktails.

Makes 20

110g/4oz/²/₃ cup of quick-cook polenta
½ teaspoon of salt
350ml/11 fl. oz/1¼ cups of boiling water
25g/1oz of melted (DF) margarine
1 teaspoon of sesame oil

A little (GF) chilli sauce/oil to taste
25g/1oz/¼ cup of sesame seeds

Grease 2–3 non-stick baking sheets with a little
    margarine

Set the oven at 180°C/350°F/Gas mark 4.

Put the polenta into a heatproof bowl with the salt and pour over the boiling water. Stir vigorously until it is smooth and then add the margarine, oil and chilli sauce. It should be the consistency of thick cream. Add a little more water if necessary.

Spoon a tablespoon of the batter on to the sheet and spread into a circle. Make about 5 per sheet. Sprinkle with the seeds and bake in batches for about 20 minutes or until the edges are just brown and crispy.

Transfer them to cool on wire racks until they are crispy and ready to eat.

Stem Ginger Cookies

Grown-up ginger cookies that have a habit of disappearing before they even get to the cookie jar!

Makes 24

100g/3½oz/½ cup of (DF) margarine
100g/3½oz/½ cup of caster (superfine) sugar
3 level tablespoons of black treacle (molasses)
3 level tablespoons of golden (corn) syrup
1 large free-range egg, beaten
75g/2½oz/½ cup of rice flour
200g/7oz/1⅓ cups of buckwheat flour
2 teaspoons of bicarbonate of soda (baking soda)

2 teaspoons each of ground ginger and ground
  cinnamon
¼ teaspoon of salt
5 tablespoons of water
5 pieces of stem ginger, finely chopped

Grease 3 baking sheets

Preheat the oven to 200°C/400°F/Gas mark 6.

Cream the margarine and sugar together until light and fluffy. Beat in the treacle (molasses), syrup, egg and remaining ingredients.
Drop half tablespoons of the mixture 5cm/2" apart on the baking sheets and bake for 6–8 minutes.
Remove the cookies from the sheets and allow to cool on a wire rack.

Coconut Crunches

These are wonderful with sorbets, or just with afternoon tea or coffee.

Serves 6–10

150g/5oz/1¾ cups of desiccated coconut
3 egg whites
3 tablespoons of caster (superfine) sugar

1 tablespoon of (GF) cornflour (cornstarch)
1 teaspoon of orange flower water

Set the oven at 180°C/350°F/Gas mark 4.

Mix all of the ingredients together to form a firm paste.
Using a spoon and your fingers, shape the dough into walnut size balls and place then on a non-stick baking sheet. Bake in the middle of the oven for 10 minutes and then reduce the heat to 150°C/300°F/Gas mark 2 and bake for a further 5 minutes.
Cool on a wire rack and store in an airtight container until needed.

Spanish Orange Cake

You can make a chocolate orange cake with this recipe by replacing 30g/1oz of the ground almonds with 30g/1oz of cocoa powder. Dust with cocoa powder mixed with icing (confectioner's) sugar for decoration.

Serves 6

3 large sweet oranges
260g/9oz/1⅓ cups of caster (superfine) sugar
6 large free-range eggs, separated
350g/12oz/4 cups of ground almonds
2 teaspoons of ground cinnamon
A pinch of salt

Icing (confectioner's) sugar and ground cinnamon to decorate
1 packet of cinnamon sticks

Grease and line a 23cm/9" deep round loose-bottomed cake tin with a little sunflower oil and greaseproof (wax) paper.

Set the oven at 180°C/350°F/Gas mark 4.

Put the whole, unpeeled oranges in a heavy-based pan and cover with cold water. Bring slowly to the boil and simmer for 2 hours, topping up with more water if necessary. Drain the oranges and leave to cool for 20 minutes. Cut the oranges in half and discard any pips.

Liquidize the oranges in a food processor with the sugar, egg yolks, almonds and ground cinnamon. Transfer the mixture into a large mixing bowl.

In a separate bowl whisk the egg whites and salt until stiff, but not dry. Gradually fold in the orange mixture with a metal spoon. Spoon into the cake tin and bake for 1½ hours, or until the cake is firm to the touch.

Leave to cool in the cake tin and then turn onto a plate.

Mix some cinnamon with icing (confectioner's) sugar, and dust the cake with it. Serve, decorated with a little bundle of cinnamon sticks in the centre of the cake.

Double Sticky Gingerbread

Cakes baked with treacle (molasses) or honey will last for weeks in a tin, so are useful for big families.

Serves 6

125g/4oz/³/₄ cup of rice flour
100g/3¹/₂oz/²/₃ cup of buckwheat flour
1 level teaspoon of bicarbonate of soda
  (baking soda)
1 tablespoon of ground ginger
1 tablespoon of ground mixed (pie) spice
1 teaspoon of crushed cardamom seeds
100g/3¹/₂oz/¹/₂ cup of (DF) margarine
50g/2oz/¹/₄ cup of soft brown sugar

130g/4¹/₂oz/¹/₃ cup of black treacle (molasses)
130g/4¹/₂oz/¹/₃ cup of golden (corn) syrup
2 large free-range eggs, beaten
200ml/7fl. oz/³/₄ cup of soya natural yoghurt (or
  goat's yoghurt which is not DF)

Grease a 19cm/7¹/₂" square cake tin and line it with
  greaseproof (wax) paper.

Preheat the oven to 170°C/325°F/Gas mark 3.

Sift the flours, bicarbonate of soda (baking soda), ginger, spice and cardamom seeds together in a mixing bowl.
Put the margarine, sugar, treacle (molasses) and syrup into a saucepan and warm over a low heat until the treacle and syrup have melted and the sugar has dissolved.
When the mixture has cooled, beat in the eggs. Pour this mixture into the flour. Add the yoghurt and beat with a wooden spoon to a smooth batter. Pour the batter into the tin and bake for 1¹/₄ hours. Cool for 15 minutes in the tin and then transfer to a wire rack. When cold, store in an airtight container until needed.

Christmas Cake

The longer this cake is kept the more succulent it will be, but do store it for at least a month. Baste with brandy from time to time and keep wrapped in foil, in an airtight container.

Serves 20

CAKE
500g/17oz/3½ cups of raisins
400g/14½oz/3 cups of dried currants
150g/5oz/1⅓ cups of dried pineapple, chopped
150g/5oz/¾ cup of glacé cherries
150g/5oz/1 cup of dried figs, chopped
150g/5oz/¾ cup of candied citrus peel, chopped
(DF) sunflower margarine for greasing paper
175g/6oz/1¼ cups of white rice flour
200g/7oz/2 cups of brown rice flour
¼ teaspoon of salt
½ teaspoon of mixed (pie) spice
1 teaspoon of grated nutmeg

2 teaspoons of ground allspice
365g/12oz/1½ cups of (DF) margarine
375g/12½oz/1¾ cups of brown sugar
6 large free-range eggs
6 tablespoons of brandy

ICING
4–5 tablespoons of smooth apricot jam (jelly)
Icing (confectioner's) sugar for rolling
500g/17oz of (GF) golden marzipan
1kg/2.2lb of ready-made-to-roll (GF) white icing
Ribbon, decorations or food colouring (optional)

Preheat the oven to 150°C/300°F/Gas mark 2.

Put the fruit in a bowl and cover with boiling water. Leave until tepid, then drain. Meanwhile, grease and line a 25cm/10" cake tin with a double layer of greaseproof (wax) paper and then grease the paper.
Sift the flours with the salt, mixed (pie) spice, nutmeg and allspice. Cream the margarine and sugar together in a big bowl until soft and light (or use a food processor and then return the mixture to the bowl). Add 1 egg at a time, beating it into the mixture. When you have added all the eggs, mix in the flour mixture in several batches. Finally, add the brandy and dried fruits. Spoon the batter into the tin and smooth the top, hollowing the centre slightly. Bake for 3 hours or until cooked through. (Insert a skewer into the cake – it is ready if the skewer comes out clean. Test in several places.) If the cake browns too quickly cover loosely with foil.
Leave to cool in the tin and then unmould and peel off the paper. Wrap the cake in foil and store. The week you intend to eat the cake, unwrap it and place on a cake board. Gently heat the apricot jam (jelly) and brush it all over the cake. Sprinkle a work surface with icing (confectioner's) sugar and roll out the marzipan with a rolling pin, using it to lift the marzipan over the cake and cover it. Trim off any excess and press closely into the cake. Trim again if necessary. Leave for 24 hours in a cool place to dry out. Roll out the ready-made icing in the same way, cover and trim. Decorate and store until needed in an airtight container.

Cranberry Date Loaf

Cranberry Date Loaf is delicious on its own or slightly buttered. You can use whatever dried fruit you happen to have.

Makes about 10 slices

75g/2¹/₂oz/¹/₃ cup of dried cranberries
75g/2¹/₂oz/¹/₃ cup of dried cherries
75g/2¹/₂oz/¹/₂ cup of dried chopped dates
125ml/4fl. oz/¹/₂ cup of black china tea
The grated rind of 1 orange
3 tablespoons of orange juice
150g/5oz/²/₃ cup of pear or apple purée, unsweetened
150g/5oz/1 cup of potato flour
100g/3¹/₂oz/³/₄ cup of rice flour
1 heaped teaspoon of cream of tartar

1 teaspoon of bicarbonate of soda (baking soda)
150g/5oz/²/₃ cup of (DF) margarine
100g/3¹/₂oz/1 cup of ground almonds
75g/2¹/₂oz/1 cup of flaked almonds
1 egg, beaten
75g/2¹/₂oz/¹/₂ cup of carrot, grated
2 teaspoons mixed (pie) spice

1kg/2.2lb loaf tin, greased and lined with greaseproof (wax) paper

Set the oven at 180°C/350°F/Gas mark 4.

Mix the fruit with the boiling hot tea, orange rind and juice in a bowl and leave to cool. Add the fruit purée and blend in.
In another bowl, sift the flours and mix in the cream of tartar and bicarbonate of soda (baking soda). Then, with a blunt ended knife, mix in the margarine until it resembles crumbs. Add the ground almonds and half the flaked almonds, the fruit with its liquid, egg, carrot and spice. Spoon into the tin and sprinkle with the remaining flaked almonds.
Cover loosely with foil and bake for 50 minutes or until an inserted skewer comes out clean. Cool and turn out onto a rack until cold. Serve in slices.

Banana and Lemon Iced Loaf

Over-ripe bananas needn't go to waste again. You can whip up this cake and freeze it if no one is around to appreciate it!

Serves 6

150g/5oz/1 cup of rice flour
150g/5oz/1 cup of buckwheat flour
3 heaped teaspoons of (GF) baking powder
½ teaspoon of salt
250g/8½oz/1 cup of (DF) margarine
250g/8½oz/1¼ cups of sugar

650g/23oz of bananas, peeled and mashed
4 large free-range eggs
4 tablespoons sifted icing (confectioner's) sugar
½–1 tablespoon lemon juice

23–25cm/9"–10" loaf tin, greased and lined

Preheat the oven to 180°C/350°F/Gas mark 4.

Sift the flours into a bowl with the baking powder and salt.
In a food processor beat the margarine, sugar and bananas together until smooth and then briefly blend in the eggs. Stir this into the flour mixture until it is evenly blended.
Pour into the loaf tin and bake for about 1–1¼ hours or until an inserted skewer comes out clean and the cake is just firm. (If it browns too quickly, cover the tin loosely with foil).
Cool in the tin for 10 minutes and then transfer to a wire rack.
When it is cold, mix the icing (confectioner's) sugar with enough of the lemon juice to make a thick enough paste to drizzle over the cake. Store in an airtight container until needed.

Almond Shortbread

This shortbread can be served with any (DF) ice cream or a bowl of poached fruit, or just with a cup of espresso as a treat!

Serves 6–12

225g/8oz/1 cup of caster (superfine) sugar
225g/8oz/2½ cups of ground almonds
225g/8oz/1½ cups of instant quick-cook polenta
225g/8oz/1 cup of (DF) margarine
1 teaspoon of almond essence

2 x 20cm/8" loose bottomed fluted flan tins

Preheat the oven to 170°C/325°F/Gas mark 3.

Mix all of the dry ingredients in a bowl. Mix in the margarine and almond essence until well blended. Press into the tin and spread evenly.
Bake for 25 minutes until golden and firm to the touch. Cool in the tin and then turn out onto a wire rack. Store in an airtight container until needed.

CHAPTER 10

Scones, Muffins and Breads

Walnut and Sage Scones

This is a very quick alternative to bread and makes up for not being able to eat things like pitta bread or the focaccia that I used to serve with soups. You can freeze the scones and reheat them briefly in the microwave for parties. They are delicious sprinkled with grated sheep's or goat's cheese, if you can tolerate dairy products.

Serves 8

125g/4oz/³/₄ cup of rice flour
100g/3¹/₂oz/²/₃ cup of buckwheat flour
50g/1³/₄oz of (DF) margarine
¹/₄ teaspoon of (GF) chilli sauce/oil
100g/3¹/₂oz/1 cup of roughly chopped walnuts
15g/¹/₂oz/¹/₂ cup of chopped fresh sage leaves or
    1 tablespoon of dried sage leaves

1 egg and unsweetened apple juice to make the
    mixture up to 175ml/6fl. oz/³/₄ cup
2 teaspoons of (GF) baking powder
1 teaspoon of bicarbonate of soda (baking soda)
¹/₄ teaspoon of salt

Set the oven to 220°C/425°F/Gas mark 7.

Grease and flour a large baking sheet.
Sift the flours and mix with the margarine and chilli sauce in a bowl. Rub gently with your floured fingertips until the mixture resembles breadcrumbs and then add the walnuts and sage. Mix in well.
Beat the egg with the juice. Gently add the baking powder, bicarbonate of soda (baking soda) and salt to the walnut mixture. Quickly mix in the liquid and briefly knead into a dough.
Roll out on a floured board into a 3.5cm/1¹/₂" thick circle. Using a 5cm/2" cutter, cut out 8 scones and dust with flour or sprinkle with a suitable hard cheese if desired.
Bake for 10–15 minutes until brown and well risen.
Serve warm or cool on wire rack and freeze until needed.

Chilli and Herb Corn Bread

This is the best recipe I know for corn bread and it can be used to accompany soups, casseroles and salads. To make this into a sweet bread, substitute the 100g/3½oz of sweetcorn for the same amount of sultanas or pine nuts and omit the chilli and herbs, using the grated rind of one lemon instead.

Serves 6–8

75g/2½oz/½ cup of rice flour
75g/2½oz/½ cup of maize flour/meal
140g/5oz/1 cup of instant polenta
1 tablespoon of (GF) baking powder
¾ teaspoon of salt
2 teaspoons of runny honey
2 large free-range eggs
300ml/10fl. oz/1¼ cups of soya milk
3 tablespoons of corn oil
A few drops of (GF) chilli sauce/oil

120g/4oz/⅔ cup of either chopped sweetcorn kernels or chopped olives and sun-dried tomatoes or 120g/4oz/⅔ cup of cooked chopped onion or bacon
1 mild chilli pepper, seeded and chopped
1 tablespoon of chopped herbs, either thyme, parsley, sage or chives
Poppy seeds to decorate

A large loaf tin, greased and lined with baking parchment

Preheat the oven to 200°C/400°F/Gas mark 6.

Sieve and mix the dry ingredients into a bowl.
In another bowl, whisk the honey, eggs, milk, oil and chilli sauce with the chopped sweetcorn, or whatever you have chosen.
Add the chilli pepper and herbs and mix together well. Stir this into the flours.
Pour the batter into the prepared tin, sprinkle with poppy seeds and bake for 35 minutes, or until an inserted skewer comes out clean.
Serve in thick slices.

Cumin Seed and Rye Bread

This recipe makes 2 loaves so you can pop one into the deep freeze. You can use any sort of seeds that you like.

Makes 2 loaves

450g/16oz/3¼ cups of rye flour
300g/11oz/2 cups of white rice flour
1 teaspoon of salt
14g/½oz of easy-bake (instant) yeast
300ml/10fl. oz/1¼ cups of unsweetened apple juice
   mixed in equal parts with water to blood
   temperature

2 tablespoons of black treacle (molasses)
1 tablespoon of cumin seeds

2 greased non-stick loaf tins

Set the oven to 200°C/400°F/Gas mark 6.

Sift together the flours and salt in a bowl. Mix in the yeast and make a well in the dry ingredients, then stir in the warm apple juice and water mixture.
Dip a tablespoon into boiling water to heat it and then use the spoon to add the treacle (molasses) to the warm mixture and mix until you have a firm dough.
Knead thoroughly on a lightly floured surface for 10 minutes. Divide the mixture into 2 non-stick loaf tins, cover with clingfilm (plastic wrap), and leave in a warm place until the dough has doubled in size.
Place the tins on a baking sheet.
Sprinkle the bread tops with a little water and then the cumin seeds.
Bake in the oven for 45 minutes. Remove from the oven to cool slightly before leaving on a wire rack to cool completely.
Serve cold in slices or freeze until needed.

Date and Pecan Muffins

This is a lovely winter muffin, warming, sweet and filling to bolster you up for a cold morning.

Serves 6–12

175g/6oz/1¼ cups of rice flour
175g/6oz/1¼ cups of buckwheat flour
2 level teaspoons of (GF) baking powder
1 teaspoon of bicarbonate of soda (baking soda)
150g/5oz/¾ cup of muscovado sugar
200g/7oz/1½ cups of dates, chopped

150g/5oz/1⅓ cups of chopped pecans
1 heaped teaspoon of mixed (pie) spice
2 large free-range eggs
300ml/10fl. oz/1¼ cups of apple juice
1 teaspoon of Madagascan vanilla essence
100g/3½oz/½ cup of (DF) margarine, melted

Set the oven at 200°C/400°F/Gas mark 6.

Sieve and then mix together all the dry ingredients, adding the dates, pecans and spice. Beat the eggs, apple-juice, vanilla essence and margarine together until frothy. Blend briefly into the flour. Spoon into paper-lined deep muffin tins and bake in the oven for 15–20 minutes until well-risen and spongy to touch. Serve warm.

Cinnamon, Honey and Oat Bread

This is a good emergency bread as I always have porridge oats at home but I often run out of the various kinds of flours needed for wheat free bread. You can vary it by adding chopped nuts, seeds or raisins.

Serves 8

7g/¼oz of easy-bake (instant) yeast

1 teaspoon of salt

2 tablespoons of honey

400ml/14fl. oz/1½ cups of warm water

1 tablespoon of vegetable oil

500g/16½oz/6 cups of porridge oats, processed
   finely to a flour

2 heaped teaspoons of cinnamon powder

1–2 tablespoons of seeds or chopped nuts or some
   sultanas

2 greased non-stick loaf tins

Set the oven at 180°C/350°F/Gas mark 4.

Put the yeast, salt and honey together in the warm water with the oil in a big bowl and then mix in the processed oats and cinnamon.

Add any nuts, seeds or sultanas and then knead with floured hands on a floured board for 10 minutes.

Divide the dough in two and shape to fit into the tins. Prove for about 30 minutes, allowing the dough to rise slightly. Bake for 1 hour or until the bread is firm.

Cool on a wire rack and then slice to serve.

Corn and Blueberry Muffins

If you can't buy blueberries you can use bilberries or just swop around fruit to suit availability. You can also used dried fruit such as cranberries or cherries.

Serves 6–12

250g/8¹/₂oz/1³/₄ cups of rice flour

2 teaspoons of (GF) baking powder

1 teaspoon of bicarbonate of soda (baking soda)

185g/6oz/1¹/₃ cups of instant polenta

2 tablespoons of sugar

225g/8oz/1²/₃ cups of frozen, fresh or dried blueberries

185g/6oz/³/₄ cup of soya yoghurt with live ferments (or goat's yoghurt, which is not DF)

2 tablespoons of lemon juice

The grated rind of 1 lemon

1 tablespoon of corn oil

250g/8¹/₂oz/1¹/₄ cups of crushed pineapple (in natural juice)

Apple juice to moisten

1 × 12 non-stick muffin tray, greased

Preheat the oven to 200°C/400°F/Gas mark 6.

Sift the flour, baking powder and bicarbonate of soda (baking soda) into a bowl. Stir in the polenta, sugar and blueberries and mix thoroughly.

Mix the yoghurt, lemon juice and grated rind, corn oil and crushed pineapple in another bowl. Pour the liquid into the dry ingredients and briefly stir in.

Add just enough apple juice to make the batter soft and easy to spoon into the moulds. Place spoonfuls of the mixture into the tin and bake for about 15 minutes, or until golden brown and spongy to touch.

Leave in the tray for 5 minutes to cool and then transfer them to a wire rack until they are ready to eat.

My List of Ingredients

Lately the biggest modern blight that disrupts social occasions is the ever-increasing list of food intolerance endured by children and adults of all ages. My recipes feature many familiar ingredients, but also staple foods such as soya products that you might normally hesitate to buy. This list might come in useful.

MY LIST

Cold pressed olive oil and good quality sunflower oil.

Unsweetened apple juice and carrot juice.

Jar of dairy free pesto sauce and a jar of tahini.

Ground almonds and walnuts.

Cold pressed organic honey and sugar free jams (jellies).

(GF) chilli sauce/oil, soya sauce, (GF) Worcestershire sauce.

(DF) luxury dark chocolate.

Soya milk and soya cream.

Coconut milk and cream.

Tomor vegetarian margarine, pure sunflower or soya margarine.

Frozen ice cream dessert (Swedish glacé or Tofutti).

Marsala, dry white vermouth and Amaretto liqueur.

Instant polenta.

Oats, buckwheat flour, white rice flour.

(GF) cornflour (cornstarch), potato flour.

Wheat free and gluten free baking powder and bicarbonate of soda (baking soda).

Wild, arborio, brown and pudding rice.

Rice, corn and buckwheat spaghetti and pasta shapes.

Large free-range eggs.

Unrefined brown Mauritian sugar.

Mixed dried fruits and pulses.

Marigold yeast free and gluten free vegetable stock powder.

Fresh garlic, ginger, lemons and limes.

Tofu.

Symbols Used Throughout This Book

The following symbols have been used to make sure that you can use each recipe with total confidence.
A professional nutritionist has checked each recipe.

 GF = Gluten free (which is wheat free).

 WF = Wheat free (which is not gluten free. However, check the recipe because you may be able to tolerate oats or barley).

 DF = Dairy free (this is lactose free. All non-dairy free recipes use goat's or sheep's products which can be tolerated by most people).

INGREDIENTS THAT SHOULD BE AVOIDED BY PEOPLE SUFFERING DAIRY, GLUTEN OR SUGAR INTOLERANCE

Dairy	**Gluten**	**Sugar**
Butter	Durum wheat (pasta)	Some sweeteners
Buttermilk	Barley	Honey
Cheese	Semolina	Fructose
Cream	Sausages	Sugar
Ghee	Malt	Maltose
Hydrolyzed whey protein	Oats	Golden syrup
Lactose	Wheat flour	Invert syrup
Margarine or shortening containing whey	Bran	Glucose (inc. glucose syrup)
	Prepared stuffing	Molasses
Milk solids	Starch (inc. modified starch)	Maple syrup
Non-milk fat solids	Rusk	Treacle
Skimmed milk powder	Rye	Dextrose
Whey	Whisky	Corn syrup
Yoghurt		Malt syrup
		Sucrose

As butter is tastier and may be healthier when heated than many margarines, we recommend using butter in place of margarine in these recipes if you can tolerate it. **However, do not try this unless you are sure you are able to tolerate butter.**

Please note that unless otherwise stated, pint measurements refer to English, not American pints (20fl.oz, not 16fl.oz).

Useful Addresses

ORGANIZATIONS

UK

Action Against Allergy
24–26 High Street
Hampton Hill
Middlesex TW1 1PD
Tel: 0181 892 2711

Coeliac Society
P O Box 220
High Wycombe
Buckinghamshire HP11 2HY
Tel: 01494 437 278

IBS Network
Centre for Human Nutrition
Northern General Hospital
Sheffield S5 7AU
Tel: 0114 261 1531

Institute for Optimum
Nutrition
Blades Court
Deodar Road
London SW15 2NU
Tel: 0181 877 9993

Myalgic Encephalomyelitis
(ME) Association
PO Box 87
Stanford-le-Hope
Essex SS17 8EX
Tel: 01375 642 466

National Eczema Society
163 Evershalt Street
London NW1 1BU
Tel: 0171 388 4097

British Heart Foundation
14 Fitzhardinge Street
London W1H 4DH
Tel: 0171 935 0185

Nutrition Associates
Galtres House
Lysander Close
Clifton Moregate
York YO3 OXB
Tel: 01904 691 591

Vegetarian Society
Parkdale
Dunham Road
Altrincham
Cheshire WA14 4QG
Tel: 0161 928 0793

USA

Allergy Resources Inc.
PO Box 888
Palmer Lake
CO 80133
Tel: 1 800 873 3529

American Allergy
Association
PO Box 7273
Menlo Park
CA 94026
Tel: 415 322 1663

American Celiac Society
Dietary Support Coalition
Ms Annette Bentley
58 Musano Court
West Orange
NJ 07052

Asthma and Allergy
Foundation of America
1717 Massachusetts Avenue
Suite 305
Washington DC 20036
Tel: 202 265 0265

Gluten Intolerance Group
PO Box 23053
Seattle
WA 98102
Tel: 206 854 9606

UK

Allergy Care
9 Corporation Street
Taunton
Somerset TA1 4AJ
Tel: 01823 325 023
Allergy-free ingredients.

D & D Specialist Chocolates
Berrydale House
5 Lawn Road
London NW3 2XS
Tel: 0171 722 2866
Chocolates and seasonal
novelties. Gluten, dairy, sugar
or cocoa free.

Farm-a-round
Tel: 0181 291 4519
Organic fruit and vegetables
delivered to your door.

H R Higgins Ltd
79 Duke Street
London W1M 6AS
Tel: 0171 629 3913
Specialist coffee supplier.

Wholefood Organically
Grown Produce
24 Paddington Street
London W1M 4DR

USA

Arrowhead Mills Inc.
Box 2059
Hereford TX 79045
Tel: 800 749 0730
Fax: 806 364 8242
Mail order suppliers of grains,
flours, pulses (legumes), cereals
and seeds.

Bob's Red Mill Natural
Foods Inc.
5209 S.E. International Way
Milwauke
OR 97222
Tel: 503 654 3215
Fax: 503 653 1339
Mail order stockists of grains,
flours, pulses (legumes),
cereals & seeds.

Ener-g Foods Inc.
PO Box 84487
Seattle
WA 98124–5787
Tel: 800 331 5222
Fax: 206 764 3398
Suppliers of food allergy
products, many rice-based,
including rice flours, rice pasta,
egg replacer, almond milk mix
as well as baked goods.

Gold Mine Natural Food Co.
3419 Hancock Street
San Diego
CA 92110–4307
Tel: 800 475 3663
Fax: 619 296 9756

Stockist of rice, barley and
other organic grains and seeds.
Jaffe Brothers Natural Foods
PO Box 636
Valley Center
CA 92082 0636
Tel: 616 749 1133
Fax: 619 749 1282
Wholefood suppliers of nuts,
nut butters, dried fruits and
grains.

Mast Enterprises
265 North Fourth Street, # 616
Coeur D'Alene
ID 83814
Tel: 208 772 8213

Mountain Ark Trader
PO Box 3170
Fayetteville
AR 72701
Tel: 800 647 8909
Fax: 501 442 7191
Suppliers of grains and 100%
buckwheat noodles,
Japanese-style silken tofu, soy
milk and rice milk.

Walnut Acres Organic Farms
Penns Creek
PA 17862
Tel: 800 433 3998
Fax: 717 837 1146

My Selection of Menus

Christmas Day (for 8 people)

Smoked Salmon Turbans

Cumin Seed and Rye Bread

Chestnut Stuffed Turkey with Bread Sauce and Cranberry Sauce

Nutty Vegetable Roulade (v)

Roast Squash, Chestnuts and Sweet Potatoes

Mince Pies and Ginger Custard

Christmas Pudding and Zabaglione

New Year's Eve (for 8 people)

Winter Smoked Bacon Soup

Walnut and Sage Scones

Venison and Pickled Walnut Casserole

Exotic Pea Purée

Sweet Potato and Orange Purée

Chestnut and Chocolate Roulade

Easter Sunday Lunch (for 8 people)

Mexican Black Bean Soup

Chilli and Herb Corn Bread

Orange Stuffed Lamb

Honey Glazed Turnips

Celeriac Dauphinoise

Chocolate Sachetorte

Dinner Party *(for 4 people)*

Roast Artichoke, Fennel and Onion Salad

Steamed Cod on Mint Purée

Hot Chocolate Soufflé

Dinner Party *(for 6 people)*

Tomato Mousse and Avocado Ceviche

Pork Chops with Lemon and Walnut Fettuccini

Pear Tart Tatin

Anniversary Buffet *(for 16 people)*

2 × Potato Skins and Hummus Dip

2 × Smoked Mackerel Pâté

1 × Chicken in Red Pesto Sauce

2 × Spinach and Rice Torte

1 × Black Bean, Olive and Egg Salad

2 × Pearl Barley Salad

2 × Summer Fruit Mousse

Index of Recipes

Index

wild rice:
   and smoked trout blinis 14
   and water chestnut salad 73
winter smoked bacon soup 4

yeast ix
yoghurt x

zabaglione 77